ENOTECA

ENOTECA

SIMPLE, DELICIOUS RECIPES IN THE

ITALIAN WINE BAR TRADITION

JOYCE GOLDSTEIN

photographs by Angela Wyant

Wine Notes by Evan Goldstein, M.S.

CHRONICLE BOOKS

SAN FRANCISCO

First Chronicle Books LLC paperback edition, published in 2005.

ISBN 0-8118-4737-3

The Library of Congress has cataloged the previous edition as follows:
Goldstein, Joyce Esersky.
    Enoteca : simple, delicious recipes in the Italian wine bar tradition / by Joyce Goldstein ;
    wine notes by Evan Goldstein ; photographs by Angela Wyant.
        p. cm.
        ISBN 0-8118-2825-5
        Cookery, Italian. I. Goldstein, Evan. II. Title.
    TX723 .G628 2001
    641.5945—dc21   00-0664457

Manufactured in China.

Designed by DINNICK & HOWELLS
Typesetting by DINNICK & HOWELLS
Food and Prop Styling by Christine Masterson
The photographer wishes to thank Corti Brothers, Sacramento, CA; Luna Garcia; Owen Masterson

Distributed in Canada by
Raincoast Books
9050 Shaughnessy Street
Vancouver, British Columbia V6P 6E5

10 9 8 7 6 5 4 3 2 1

Chronicle Books LLC
85 Second Street
San Francisco, California 94105

www.chroniclebooks.com

TABLE OF CONTENTS

HERE'S TO SLOW FOOD, OLD WAYS, AND
LASTING FRIENDSHIPS

"Food history is as important as a baroque church. Governments should recognize cultural heritage and protect traditional foods. A cheese is as worthy of preserving as a sixteenth-century building."

Carlo Petrini, president of Slow Food

Introduction

EVOLUTION OF THE ENOTECA

MANY OBSERVERS have come to believe that 24/7, the all-day, every-day lifestyle, is a contemporary phenomenon, but in ancient Rome, wine shops, called *tavernae vinariae*, were open around the clock. Obviously, wine was an important part of the daily routine of the citizenry and not an intellectual or esoteric pursuit.

The ancient ruins at Ostia Antica, just outside of Rome, reveal what used to be a block-square apartment house on the via Diana (so-named because a statue of the goddess Diana was discovered there). In one corner of the building, almost totally intact, is an early Roman enoteca, or wine bar. It is so well preserved that, with a little tasteful remodeling and some modern plumbing, it could be reopened for business by a savvy entrepreneur. The main bar fronted directly onto the street, so that passersby could easily stop for a glass of wine. There were basins for washing dishes and glassware, and even a counter on which to dis-play wine and food. On one wall is a painting of the food that was available, an early Roman version of the blackboard menu. Fast forward to today and Terminal A at Rome's nearby Fiumicino Airport. Hungry travelers waiting for a flight can stop at the Enoteca Frescobaldi for a glass of wine and some appetizers ordered from a blackboard menu. Thus, the tradition continues.

Two well-respected enoteca guidebooks, Veronelli and Alexa, list about five hundred separate operations, in all their many permutations, located throughout Italy. Prosit, the Internet site of an enoteca-marketing group called *Gli Angoli del Buon Bere*, "Corners of Good Drink," has over four hundred members. Clearly, the enoteca is popular. But what is it? It's not a three-star restaurant with an incredible international wine cellar, such as the inappropriately named Enoteca Pinchiorri in Florence. Might the enoteca be related to the *osteria*, which was, in earlier times, a small rustic inn offering rooms to rent along with wine and simple food? Indeed, many enotecas have evolved from the older *osterie*. The oldest wine bar in Italy, and probably in all of Europe (it is listed in the *Guinness Book of Records*), is the Enoteca Al Brindisi in Ferrara. It was established in 1453 as Hostaria della Chiucchiolino (The Drunkard), and among its celebrated habitués were poets Lodovico Ariosto and Torquato Tasso, sculptor Benvenuto Cellini, and the great astronomer Copernicus. Under the direction of Maurizia Golvoni and Federico Pellegrino, it's still a good spot for a glass of wine.

Today, the term *osteria* or *locanda* refers to a casual establishment serving wine and food, sometimes at communal tables, usually in the countryside or in small towns. The enoteca is the urban counterpart, offering wines and sometimes food but in an even more abbreviated setting: no rooms to let, often no kitchen, and maybe a few tables. It may be just a wine shop with a tasting bar, or it may also offer small plates to accompany the wine selections. In its simplest configuration, an enoteca is a shop that sells wine by the bottle and serves it by the glass as well. It most likely carries a small selection of local artisanal products such as olive oils; vinegars; honeys; vegetables *sott'olio* (under oil); packaged dry pasta, grains, and lentils and other dried legumes; bottled pasta sauces, conserves, and savory condiments; and local sweets such as *panforte* in Siena, *cantucci* in Florence, and marzipan in Sicily.

The ancient Greeks called Italy *Enotria*, "the Land of the Vine," and the word *enoteca* carries a Greek origin as well. It means "to keep" or "to take care of wine." In Verona in 1990, during the twenty-fourth meeting of Vinitaly, a wine exposition, the *Associazione Internazionale Enoiteche* was formed. Why the added *i* in enoteca? The idea was to relate it back to its Greek roots, *oichia* meaning "house," *oinoiche* meaning "wine house." The association wanted to differentiate the traditional term *enoteca*, a store that bottles wine or sells wine by the bottle to take away, from an *enoiteca*, a store that sells quality wines selected by the owner or host, with wines to be tasted there or purchased to take home. In other words, the latter is a wine bar that may also be a wine shop. Habits are hard to break, so most people have overlooked this subtle spelling refinement and continue to use the more familiar enoteca. (In Italian, the plural of enoteca is *enoteche*. But, like the word *trattoria*, whose Italian plural is *trattorie*, once a term becomes popular, the correct Italian is often lost outside of Italy. The word is typically anglicized, and an *s* is added to indicate more than one. So *trattorie* becomes trattorias, *pizze* become pizzas, and, in this book, the plural of enoteca will be enotecas, as these wine bars are now part of the mainstream.)

To be a member of the *Associazione Internazionale Enoiteche*, the shop must carry at least one hundred different wines and represent at least ten different regions of Italy, five regions of France, and two other regions from outside Italy and France. Seventy percent of these wines must come directly from small producers and growers. The shop also must have five kinds of grappa and one brandy, and from time to time offer a tasting of twenty-four wines in one category. Appropriate glasses are required for each type of wine, from flutes for sparkling wine to special glasses for grappas and brandy.

The proprietors and staff who run these enotecas are not always accredited sommeliers. They are, however, enthusiastic and knowledgeable and are delighted to have you stop in to sample a few well-chosen (by them) wines and to try their local artisanal products. They are happy to talk to you about what they pour, or will leave you to taste in quiet contemplation as you stand at the well-worn wood or marble-topped wine bar, the *bancone di mescita*. You can sample a number of wines by the glass and, to showcase the wines, small plates of finger foods are served at the counter or, with sufficient space, at small tables.

Today, many popular enotecas are expanding their horizons. Some have evolved into what we would term wine bars and offer a range of casual dining. For the most part, however, enoteca food is simple, unpretentious, and easy to prepare and serve. Wines remain at center stage, and the food is there to make them shine.

Many enotecas often lack full cooking facilities, however. In some venues, a countertop oven, toaster, microwave oven, or a few burners might make up the entire kitchen. Because of limited workspace, the menu will often consist only of tidbits such as *crostini*, *bruschette*, or pieces of aged cheese accompanied by bread drizzled with truffle oil. Some offer frittatas, *panini* and *tramezzini* (small white-bread sandwiches), *torte salate* (savory pies), focaccia, plates of smoked and cured fish, a few simple roasts or stews, and an assortment of cured meats. Outside of the neighborhood butcher shop or *salumeria*, the enoteca is where you can often find the best selection of *salumi*, local sausages, salami such as the beloved Tuscan *finocchiona*, and cured meats such as *bresaola*, prosciutto, and cured goose breasts. Most offer an array of local and some imported cheeses, from very moist and fresh to well aged. These are paired creatively with fruit and special conserves or condiments.

As few places have ample table space, and as much of what is offered is eaten standing up, most enoteca food has been prepared ahead of time, ready for quick service. Some of the delicacies might have been brought in from local specialty-food shops, or may have been made at home by the wife or sister of the proprietor and transported to the bar. In the absence of a large kitchen crew, or legions of waiters, many dishes are served on platters at room temperature. A few items may be reheated. Sometimes a short written menu or a blackboard lists the offerings. A few enotecas have full kitchens, of course, and offer a trattoria- or *osteria*-style menu, but this is a recent development.

The fact that the owners of these varied enotecas have banded together to form an association is significant. Their initial goal was to promote high-quality wine and small wine makers, creating a kind of informal wine school. But they soon recognized that the public was steering away from full-service restaurants in favor of enotecas, which delivered wine and food, lower prices, smaller portions, and a genuinely casual and lively atmosphere. The owners quickly recognized the advantage of collective publicity and greater exposure in order to entice more diners to explore this new way of eating.

At first the contemporary enoteca movement was mostly centered in the Veneto, home of the *bacaro* (another term for a wine bar, named after Bacchus, the god of wine). The Venetians stop in for an *ombra* (literally a "shadow," because gondoliers used to stand in the shadow of the Campanile in the Piazza San Marco, but now the name for a glass of wine), and sample *cicchetti*, wine bar snacks. Today, however, the popularity of the enoteca has spread throughout Italy and beyond. More and more wine bars are springing up in busy urban areas. Their burgeoning business coincides with and reflects the growing trend of casualization in dining. The enoteca is not too expensive and not very formal. You can eat as little or as much as you like. You might even be able to drop in and get a table, especially if you are a regular, or get a spot at the bar. Emilio Baldi, whose family has owned the famed and elegant Ristorante Antico Martini in Venice since 1921, explains that they opened Enoteca Vino Vino next to the restaurant in 1987, to take advantage of their extensive wine cellar and as a way to reach a greater number of diners in search of a more casual experience. He reports that it has been a success since day one. Giovanni Serrazanetti of the Cantina Bentivoglio, in Bologna, says that the enoteca-with-kitchen has created a viable alternative to the traditional restaurant.

An enoteca is a great place for people who come in alone. You can dine without a companion and not feel conspicuous. Sitting at a counter talking with others over a simple meal and glass of good wine is relaxing and congenial. In fact, the wine bar can become a "Third Place." Professor Ray Oldenburg, in his thought-provoking book *The Great Good Place*, describes the Third Place as a venue we visit regularly, where we are known, and where we meet others who are *not* just like ourselves. It is an enrichment to our lives, providing us with balance and contrast from the other two habitual places: our home and our workspace. Along with offering wine and food, the ideal Third Place offers a sense of community, conviviality, and well-being.

The interest in wine continues to grow in America. Dinners with wine makers in attendance are popular, well-attended restaurant events. Some restaurants and wine shops offer wine classes and wine tastings during the hours after work. Unfortunately, too many of us lack the time to attend such gatherings. The enoteca or American wine bar provides us with such an opportunity to learn, but in an unscheduled and unstructured manner. We can drop in at any time, no class to sign up for, no special dinner reservation to make. The enoteca gives us the opportunity to deepen our knowledge about wine—to experiment, to expand our palates, to try unfamiliar wine varietals, and to sample new wines that we might enjoy in addition to the everyday selections we usually serve at home.

In Italy, pairing wine and food is easy and unpretentious. Wine goes with food and is rarely served by itself. Not surprisingly, wine is always on the table at mealtime in the Italian home. Following this example, wine and food pairing can be equally enjoyable outside of Italy. With this book in hand, you can reproduce at home some of the very best and simplest pairings in the enoteca tradition. You only need seek out imported Italian wines, cheeses, cured meats, and other foods and at the same time draw upon the output of the booming American wine industry and of our own growing numbers of quality cheese makers, butchers, bakers, and other specialty-food producers. Indeed, by following the enoteca format of combining purchased foods and assembling plates with imagination and taste, the busy home cook can create interesting, delicious meals easily and in a short time.

To collect recipes for this book, I sent a letter to owners and sommeliers of 180 enotecas in diverse regions of Italy. I asked them to send a copy of a typical menu, if it exists, and recipes for a few of their most popular and distinctive dishes. I selected this core group to see what kind of a response I would receive. To encourage them to send the recipes or menus, I enclosed a self-addressed envelope. Although I already had collected menus and had taken extensive notes about dishes that I enjoyed in the many enotecas that I had visited, I hoped to unearth a few undiscovered gems through the mailing. As a recipe addict, I can never have enough.

Weeks went by. No response. My Italophile friends said that I would never hear from anyone: "Remember, Joyce, they are Italian." Well, even the freewheeling, laid-back Italians are changing, because I received over thirty responses. Some sent recipes, some even sent cookbooks they had written or used in their kitchens. They wrote about their enotecas and often included their family's history or involvement with wine and food. As the proud mother of a master sommelier, I was happy to see how many sons and daughters worked alongside their parents. I was even told a few love stories. Many wrote with pride about their their locally produced wines and foods and regional traditions. One correspondent told me she sent her father three times a day to a nearby trattoria to pick up freshly prepared food for her customers because she had no stove!

Not all of the recipes that I received were practical for the home cook to prepare. Either the ingredients were too difficult to find, or the instructions were too labor intensive. Who has time to make *tortelloni* at home? Great fresh noodles, elegant stuffed pastas, and gnocchi are sold in shops all over Italy, and more and more pasta shops and markets are making these available to the American home cook. So buy your pasta if you can, and I will recommend an appropriate sauce. My goal for this book is simple and easy cooking with dishes that move easily from stove to table. It is fast food in the manner of the Italian wine bar.

Most of the recipes I was sent were regional in character, which is not surprising, as the enoteca promotes the best local wine and food products. A reference to the culinary traditions of the area usually accompanied each recipe. I wish I could say that clear regional differences are being maintained all over Italy, but this is not the case. While fusion food has not taken over, some places are pushing their menu to become more modern and international. (I have seen a few trendy menu items such as *fondue chinoise* and *risotto al tamarindo*, but these seem to be aberrations.) What is happening is that Italian food is crossing regional lines. In Siena I was served a passable osso buco, a Milanese specialty, and a mediocre cannoli, a Sicilian pastry. At Enoteca Baldi in Panzano, a small town in the heart of Tuscany, I dined on a tender version of *melanzana alla parmigiana*, a southern classic, and *aristà*, a Tuscan pork roast, was accompanied with *peperonata*, another dish from the south. I suspect that such crossing of culinary borders is to satisfy the armies of tourists, and possibly to give local and regular diners a broader palette from which to choose. More often than not, however, this blurring of regional distinctions produces lackluster food.

For those of us seeking to preserve an honest regionalism in menus, I am happy to report that most of the food served in enotecas remains local and traditional. One of the reasons that I am still in love with Italy is because Italians respect their heritage. I treasure the regional diversity of Italian cooking and the passion it inspires. Many enoteca owners are members of Slow Food, a grass-roots Piedmont-based organization (located in the town of Bra, near Turin) founded by Carlo Petrini to promote biodiversity and to protect and preserve culinary treasures—foods that are in danger of obsolescence. For the most part, the owners of enotecas actively support local artisans and strive to maintain the regional character of their food. And, I say, more power to them.

Although enoteca food is regional food, it has global appeal. Most of these dishes can be successfully captured and re-created in the American kitchen. The recipes I have included are neither exotic nor difficult, and the wine notes, by my son, Evan Goldstein, a master sommelier, are simple and friendly as well, suggesting both Italian possibilities and readily available alternative selections. As an Italian might say, *Niente sorpresa, ma tante scoperto*. "Nothing surprising but so much to discover."

EVAN GOLDSTEIN'S
INTRODUCTION TO THE WINE NOTES

It goes by many names: the Italian *enoteca*, the French *bar à vin*, or the relatively recent innovation, the American wine bar. As has been noted, the roots of this institution are Italian, and the classic enoteca, with its resounding focus on wine, is the paradigm. What makes it so special is its foundation in regionalism. A *bistecca alla fiorentina* served with a young, juicy Chianti, and a sublime *fonduta* or risotto accompanied by a famed Barbera or Nebbiolo from Piedmont, are illustrative models of regional wine and food pairing.

Regionalism is revealed in how the land, environment, and soils favor certain grapes; what vegetables and grains thrive there; and whether the "meat" of the region is grazing cattle or sheep, mountain goats, or flocks of ducks. There is truth to the adage that wine and food grow up together. But what are you to do when the local match isn't available to you? It's safe and easy to "go native," but in reality, it may be impractical. Do sardines *in saor* truly taste better with a Soave from the Veneto than with any other wine? Will *lasagne alla bolognese* only work with a Sangiovese di Romagna? The answer is, of course, no. We can take comfort in knowing that wines will mimic one another globally, and that the characteristics of a wine, while lacking the identical flavor profile, can be found thousands of miles apart.

What is explored in the subsequent pages are both worlds. The salient food and wine issues of each dish will be identified, followed by two wine selections: Italian wines and alternative wines. The first will be the local Italian choices, wines that may be from within the same region as the dish, resulting in a traditional Italian pairing of wine and food. These selections will take into account the availability factors encountered in the United States. The second category will suggest similar alternative wines that will pair well with the food when the regional Italian choice is unavailable.

As with all matters of food and wine, however, you should go with your heart and your taste, not with your intellect. Don't overthink the matches, and if you have other wines that you prefer or with which you would like to experiment, do so. Wine and food pairing is supposed to be fun, to be an adventure. Your happiness at the table is what counts, and whether you find that happiness in a bottle of Italian wine, in an American wine, or even a French wine, it is the same happiness. *Buon appetito!*

Piccoli piatti fritti
FRITTERS AND FRITTATAS

Arancine di riso allo zafferano **SAFFRON RICE CROQUETTES**

Crocchette di patate **POTATO CROQUETTES**

Frittata di primavera con asparagi, aglio verde, ed erbe
**SPRINGTIME OMELET WITH ASPARAGUS, GREEN GARLIC,
AND HERBS**

Frittata con alle erbe di campagna e menta
OMELET WITH WILD GREENS AND MINT

Olive all'ascolana **MEAT-STUFFED DEEP-FRIED OLIVES**

Fiori di zucchini fritti **FRIED ZUCCHINI BLOSSOMS**

Ribollita refritto **BEAN-AND-BREAD SOUP "PANCAKE**

left: *Frittata di primavera con asparagi, aglio verde, ed erbe*
SPRINGTIME OMELET WITH ASPARAGUS, GREEN GARLIC, AND HERBS, page 26

Piccoli piatti fritti

FRITTERS AND FRITTATAS

IN A CONVENTIONAL ITALIAN COOKBOOK, the recipes in this chapter would be among the antipasti, small dishes served at the start of a meal. In a wine bar, however, you don't adhere to a formal meal structure. The entire repast might be an assortment of small plates, little tastes to accompany selected glasses of wine: a handful of fried olives, a rice croquette, or a slice of frittata, perhaps paired with a small salad or some bread or *grissini*.

Frittatas are a classic wine bar offering. Although prepared in a manner similar to that of the popular Spanish omelet known as a *tortilla*, the Italian frittata is a lighter affair. A *frittata con alle erbe di campagna e menta*, flavored with an assortment of fresh herbs, is a pale jade omelet, a celebration of greens and eggs. The *frittata di primavera con asparagi*, while a specialty of Friuli and the Veneto, may be served anywhere in Italy when springtime asparagus madness strikes. Other omelets are made with zucchini and zucchini blossoms, or artichokes and mint. They have been cooked ahead of time and hold well at room temperature. Order a slice and and it is placed on a plate, sometimes appearing solo and sometimes with a little salad or some vegetables *sott'olio*, marinated in olive oil and herbs.

Ribollita refritto demonstrates the incredible versatility of the Italian kitchen. *Ribollita* makes its debut at the table as a vegetable and bean soup, not unlike a minestrone. On the second day, bread is added and the dish emerges again, reboiled, as a hearty bread-thickened soup. In its final, and probably best, menu appearance, a ladle of the very thick leftover soup is quickly sautéed and served as a bread-soup "pancake," but not before it is anointed with a drizzle of the very best olive oil. While most soups are too liquid to show off wine well, *ribollita* is a perfect hearty dish to accompany a glass of the local Chianti.

Frying food to order seems like it would be a risky proposition for the enoteca kitchen. But, with a simple deep-fryer on the premises, fritters and croquettes are a breeze. These savory items have been assembled ahead of time and need only a few minutes in bubbling hot oil, before they are popped onto a small plate with an accompanying lemon wedge or a sprinkle of coarse salt. Such tidbits as *olive all'ascolana*, the famous meat-stuffed deep-fried olives from the Marches; *arancine di riso*, Sicilian rice croquettes; or *crocchette di patate*, the potato croquettes that are popular nearly everywhere, are instant hits with enoteca customers. So, too, is the seasonal treat of *fiori di zucchini fritti*, fried zucchini blossoms with diverse fillings. Savvy drinkers know that a sparkling wine pairs naturally with all of these fried specialties.

✳

Arancine di riso allo zafferano
SAFFRON RICE CROQUETTES

Italians are loyal to their local dining and drinking establishments. The space now
occupied by Milan's Le Cantine Isola, situated in a working-class neighborhood, has housed
an enoteca for more than a century. Manager Saria Tagliaferri sent me a few lovely recipes and
the story of the enoteca. In 1961, Giacomo Isola and his wife, Milly, took over the wine
bar and gave it their name. They were madly in love with each other and with wine, Tagliaferri
wrote, and they made the shop their life. In 1993, after many years of working alone, they
hired Giovanni Sarais to help run the place. Today, Giovanni is the owner and Luca, his son,
is the sommelier and works the counter along with his mother, Tina. There are no tables, but
Luca pampers his clients at the counter with tidbits such as potato croquettes (page 25),
meatballs (page 123), and these rice croquettes. Arancine di riso are also a favorite of sommelier
Salvatore Denaro of Enoiteca Il Bacco Felice, in the Umbrian town of Foligno, as he
comes from Sicily, the home of arancine.

Makes 12 to 16 croquettes

1½ cups water

½ teaspoon chopped saffron threads, steeped in ¼ cup hot water for 15 minutes

1 teaspoon salt, plus more to taste

1 cup Arborio rice

2 eggs

6 tablespoons grated Parmesan cheese

Freshly ground black pepper

12 to 16 small cubes fresh mozzarella or Fontina cheese

1 tablespoon chopped fresh marjoram or sage

¾ cup fine dried bread crumbs

Olive or peanut oil for deep-frying

Combine the water, saffron infusion, and salt in a saucepan and bring to a boil
over high heat. Add the rice all at once, reduce the heat to low, and cover the pan.
Simmer until the rice has absorbed all of the water and is cooked through but

still sticky, about 20 minutes. Stir in the eggs and Parmesan and season with salt and pepper.

Remove from the heat and spoon the rice out onto a baking sheet, spreading it evenly to cool it quickly. Refrigerate until cold but not hard.

To make the croquettes, first roll the cheese cubes in the marjoram or sage to coat evenly. Spread the bread crumbs on a plate. Scoop up a spoonful of the rice into your hand. With a finger, make an indentation in the rice and tuck a cube of cheese into the center. Smooth the rice over the filling, forming a round ball about 2 inches in diameter. Dip the croquettes in the bread crumbs, covering evenly, and place on a baking sheet lined with parchment paper. Repeat until all the rice is used. Refrigerate the croquettes until you are ready to fry them or for up to 24 hours. (It is easier to fry them when they are fully chilled, as they have firmed up.)

To cook the croquettes, pour the oil to a depth of 3 inches into a deep sauté pan or saucepan and heat to 350°F. Add the croquettes, a few at a time, to the hot oil and fry, lifting them out of the oil a few times so that the cheese will have time to melt in the center, until golden brown, 6 to 7 minutes. Using a slotted spoon or tongs, transfer to paper towels to drain. Keep warm in a low oven for no more than 10 to 15 minutes. Repeat until all the croquettes are cooked, then serve piping hot.

MATCHING POINTER: *While a sparking wine is an exquisite alternative, a white wine is better. The saffron offers an exotic nuance, and a suggestion of "sweetness" is delivered by the deep-frying and the rice. A slightly off-dry wine is an interesting choice, too.* ❋ **ITALIAN WINES:** CHARDONNAY (ALTO ADIGE), ORVIETO ❋ **ALTERNATIVE WINES:** SÉMILLON AND SAUVIGNON BLENDS (FRANCE), CHENIN BLANC WITH A SNAP OF SWEETNESS (FRANCE, SOUTH AFRICA, CALIFORNIA)

＊

Crocchette di patate
POTATO CROQUETTES

Here's another tidbit that Luca Sarais serves at the busy counter at
Le Cantine Isola (page 23). You can form these creamy and crunchy potato croquettes
up to 8 hours in advance and refrigerate them until it is time to fry them.

Makes about 15 croquettes

2 pounds boiling potatoes, peeled and quartered

2 whole eggs, plus 2 egg yolks

¾ cup grated Parmesan cheese

¼ cup chopped fresh chives

¼ cup chopped fresh flat-leaf parsley

Salt and freshly ground black pepper

Freshly grated nutmeg or ground mace

½ cup all-purpose flour, or as needed

1 cup fine dried bread crumbs, or as needed

Vegetable or olive oil for deep-frying

Place the potatoes in a saucepan with salted water to cover. Bring to a boil and cook until tender, about 20 minutes. Drain and pass the warm potatoes through a ricer placed over a bowl, or mash well with a hand masher. Add the whole eggs, egg yolks, cheese, chives, and parsley to the potatoes and mix well. Season well with salt, pepper, and nutmeg or mace, again mixing well. Cover and chill for about 1 hour to make the mixture easier to shape.

Spread the flour on a plate, then spread some of the bread crumbs on a second plate. To make the croquettes, scoop up some potato mixture and form into a 2-inch-long oval, or into a round if you prefer. Dip the croquette first into the flour, coating evenly, and then into the crumbs, again coating evenly. Place on a rack or on a baking sheet lined with parchment paper. Repeat until all the potato mixture is used. Refrigerate the croquettes until you are ready to fry them.

(They will hold together better if they are cold.)

To cook, pour the oil to a depth of 3 inches into a deep sauté pan or saucepan and heat to 375°F. When the oil is hot, add the croquettes, a few at a time, to the hot oil and fry until golden, about 5 minutes. Using a slotted spoon or tongs, transfer to paper towels to drain. Keep warm in a low oven for no more than 10 to 15 minutes. Repeat until all croquettes are cooked, then serve piping hot.

MATCHING POINTER: *Similar to the rice croquettes (page 23) but without the textural elements of the rice and saffron. The rich consistency requires a white wine with more body. Again, bubbles are nice, too.* ❀ **ITALIAN WINES:** CHARDONNAY (FRIULI, TUSCANY), CHARDONNAY- OR CORTESE-BASED OLTREPÒ PAVESE, STILL OR *FRIZZANTE* ❀ **ALTERNATIVE WINES:** CHABLIS (BURGUNDY), CHARDONNAY (NEW ZEALAND)

❀

Frittata di primavera con asparagi, aglio verde, ed erbe
SPRINGTIME OMELET WITH ASPARAGUS, GREEN GARLIC, AND HERBS

Italian cooks, always in thrall with the rhythms of nature, celebrate springtime by putting wild asparagus and green garlic on the menu every day they are in season. The pencil-thin, slightly bitter asparagus can be simply cooked and served alone or incorporated into an omelet. For his frittata recipe, Salvatore Denaro of the Enoiteca Il Bacco Felice in Foligno, in the region of Umbria, recommends using erbe del bosco, *or gathered wild herbs from the forest. We are not lucky enough to be able to forage in the Italian woods, so I suggest you assemble a pleasing mixture of herbs from what is available at your local market or in your garden, such as a combination of mint, flat-leaf parsley, thyme, marjoram, and tarragon. If you cannot find green garlic, use ½ cup chopped green onions in its place, sautéing them until soft but not brown, about 5 minutes. Then add 3 or 4 cloves garlic, minced, with the asparagus.*

Serves 6

6 or 7 eggs
Salt and freshly ground black pepper
5 tablespoons extra-virgin olive oil
½ cup chopped green garlic
1½ pounds pencil-thin asparagus spears, tough ends removed, blanched for
    3 minutes, drained, and cut into 1-inch pieces
½ cup chopped mixed fresh fragrant herbs (see recipe introduction)

Lightly beat the eggs in a bowl until blended. Season with salt and pepper and set aside.

Warm the olive oil in a medium-sized sauté pan over medium heat. Add the green garlic and sauté until soft, 3 to 5 minutes. Reduce the heat to low, add the asparagus and herbs, and stir for 2 minutes. Add the beaten eggs and mix well. Raise the heat to medium and cook, without stirring, until the omelet is set and golden on the bottom but the top is still runny, 8 to 10 minutes. While the omelet cooks, run a spatula around the edge of the pan a few times, to prevent sticking.

Invert a plate on top of the pan, then carefully invert the pan and plate together. Lift off the pan and slide the omelet, browned side up, back into the pan. Cook the second side over medium heat until pale gold, about 3 minutes longer. Do not overcook, as you don't want the eggs to be dry. (Alternatively, use a flameproof sauté pan and slip the omelet under a preheated broiler to brown the top.)

Slide the omelet onto a serving plate, let it cool for a bit, and then cut into wedges to serve.

MATCHING POINTER: Eggs and wine are a difficult match. A white wine with some sharp acidity is the conventional solution to overcome the egg, but a medium-bodied and slightly herbal red wine is a successful departure. ❁ **ITALIAN WINES:** BREGANZE ROSSO, MERLOT (VENETO) ❁ **ALTERNATIVE WINES:** MERLOT (SOUTHWEST FRANCE, WASHINGTON STATE, NEW ZEALAND), CABERNET FRANC (LOIRE VALLEY CHINON OR BOURGEUIL)

✻

Frittata con alle erbe di campagna e menta

OMELET WITH WILD GREENS AND MINT

The Enoteca di Cormons is a cooperative with thirty members, twenty-eight of whom are wine producers from the Comune di Cormons in Friuli. The enoteca does not have a chef, but it does have a modest kitchen in which members are able to produce simple and tasty morsels to serve with their fine selection of wines. They offer superb prosciutto, the famed San Daniele of the region, and a local one from Cormons that Lorenzo d'Osvaldo smokes over cherry wood and flavors with juniper. Enoteca manager Luisa Lucia sent this recipe for a greens frittata that is typically served with a glass of the local Sauvignon Blanc. If putting together an interesting mix of braising greens, such as dandelion, mizuna, collards, kale, frisée, and tatsoi, proves difficult, use spinach, escarole, or Swiss chard, or a combination.

Serves 4 to 6

1½ pounds assorted braising greens (see recipe introduction)

5 eggs

½ cup milk

1 tablespoon all-purpose flour

Salt and freshly ground black pepper

5 tablespoons extra-virgin olive oil

1 small onion, chopped

¼ cup chopped fresh mint

¼ cup chopped sorrel (optional)

Greens usually harbor grit and sand, so rinse them well in a sink full of cold water, swishing them around so that the dirt falls to the bottom. Use a wire skimmer to transfer the greens to a colander, then allow them to drain well. Chop the greens coarsely. Bring a saucepan filled with lightly salted water to a boil, add the greens, and boil until tender, 3 to 6 minutes. Drain in a colander, pressing out excess moisture.

Combine the eggs, milk, and flour in a bowl and beat lightly until blended. Season with salt and pepper and set aside.

Warm the olive oil in a medium-sized sauté pan over medium heat. Add the onion and sauté until soft, about 8 minutes. Add the drained greens, mint, and the sorrel, if using, and cook for a minute or two. Add the beaten eggs and mix well. Cook over medium heat, without stirring, until the omelet is set and golden on the bottom but the top is still runny, about 8 minutes. While the omelet cooks, run a spatula around the edge of the pan a few times, to prevent sticking.

Invert a plate on top of the pan, then carefully invert the pan and the plate together. Lift off the pan and slide the omelet, browned side up, back into the pan. Cook the second side over medium heat until pale gold, about 3 minutes longer. Do not overcook, as you don't want the eggs to be dry.

Slide the omelet onto a serving plate, let it cool for a bit, and then cut into wedges to serve.

MATCHING POINTER: *A young, crisp white wine with high acidity (sharpness) will play off nicely against the mint.* ❋ **ITALIAN WINES:** GAVI DI CORTESE, FIANO DI AVELLINO ❋ **ALTERNATIVE WINES:** SAUVIGNON BLANC (SOUTH AFRICA, SOUTH AMERICA), ALBARIÑO (SPAIN)

✲

Olive all'ascolana

MEAT-STUFFED DEEP-FRIED OLIVES

Ascoli, in the region of the Marches, is known for its tender giant green olives. Sommelier Nazareno Migliori and his wife, Marinella, who run the Enoteca Migliori in Ascoli Piceno, grow and process their own olives and cure their own prosciutto. Along with a fine selection of wines, they also offer a full menu. One of their specialties is an elaborate fritto misto all'ascolana, *which includes baby lamb chops, artichokes, zucchini, mushrooms, and these famous olives stuffed with a meat filling. The olives alone are an ideal small plate to serve with a glass of wine. Pitted green olives are available at the market, but some may be too small to stuff. You can, however, use those large green olives that come stuffed with pimiento or garlic. The fillings are easy to remove, and the time spent doing so will be less than pitting one hundred olives!*

Makes about 100 olives

FILLING:

2 tablespoons olive oil

1 small onion, chopped

2 carrots, peeled and chopped

2 celery stalks, chopped

¼ pound ground lean beef or veal

¾ pound ground lean pork

¼ pound ground chicken

½ cup dry white wine

2 eggs

1¼ cups grated Parmesan cheese

Freshly grated nutmeg

100 large, tender green olives, pitted

1 cup all-purpose flour

2 eggs

2 cups fine dried bread crumbs

Olive oil for deep-frying

To make the filling, warm the olive oil in a large sauté pan over medium heat. Add the onion, carrots, celery, and all the ground meats and sauté until they start to take on color, 15 to 20 minutes. Deglaze the pan with the wine, stirring to dislodge any brown bits on the pan bottom, and then put the mixture through a meat grinder or pulse in a food processor until evenly ground.

In a bowl, combine the meat mixture, eggs, Parmesan, and nutmeg to taste and mix well. If not using immediately, cover and refrigerate until you are ready to stuff the olives. (The filling will keep for up to 2 days. Bring the mixture to room temperature when you want to stuff the olives, or it may be too stiff to push through a pastry tube.)

Spoon the filling into a pastry bag fitted with a small plain tip and pipe the filling into the pitted olives. (At this point, if the filling has not been refrigerated for more than a few hours, the olives can be refrigerated up to 2 days before frying.)

To fry the olives, put the flour in a shallow bowl. Beat the eggs in another shallow bowl, and put the bread crumbs in a third bowl.

Pour the olive oil to a depth of 2 to 3 inches into a deep sauté pan or saucepan and heat to 350°F.

In batches, dip the stuffed olives in the flour, then the egg, and finally the bread crumbs, and drop them into the hot oil. Deep-fry until golden, about 4 minutes. Using a slotted spoon, transfer to paper towels to drain briefly, then serve at once.

MATCHING POINTER: One needs a crisp white to, at once, refresh the palate and provide balance against the effect of deep-frying. Look to pick up on the olive flavors, too. ✤ **ITALIAN WINES:** VERDICCHIO (CASTELLI DI JESI, MATELICA), BIANCO DI CUSTOZA ✤ **ALTERNATIVE WINES:** SAUVIGNON BLANC (NEW ZEALAND, CHILE), PINOT BLANC (FRANCE, CALIFORNIA)

❋

Fiori di zucchini fritti

FRIED ZUCCHINI BLOSSOMS

*At the Osteria del Vicolo Nuovo in Imola, just outside Bologna, these fried
zucchini blossoms filled with ricotta are among the menu offerings. The osteria, which
is also an enoteca, is set in a sixteenth-century building with vaulted ceilings.
Ambra Lenini and Rosanna Tozzoli run the front of the house, while Romana Poli is
in charge of the kitchen. In the United States, zucchini blossoms were once a special treat
reserved for home gardeners and habitués of farmers' markets. But now these showy
flowers are starting to appear in the produce section of some supermarkets. While they are
delicious cut into strips and added to a frittata or risotto, Mother Nature designed them
for stuffing. You can make a light batter for frying, or simply dip the blossoms
in beaten eggs and then in flour.*

Serves 8 to 10

16 to 20 zucchini blossoms

FILLING:

1½ cups (about ¾ pound) ricotta cheese

6 tablespoons grated Parmesan cheese

1 egg

¼ cup chopped fresh herbs such as basil, marjoram, and/or flat-leaf parsley

Salt and freshly ground black pepper

BATTER:

2 eggs

2 cups all-purpose flour

Salt and freshly ground black pepper

2 cups ice water or chilled club soda, or as needed

Olive oil for deep-frying

Coarse salt

Soak the zucchini blossoms in ice water for 30 minutes to crisp them. Drain carefully and pat dry. Alternatively, gently wipe the zucchini flowers with a damp paper towel. Carefully reach inside each flower and pinch off the stamens.

To make the filling, combine the ricotta, Parmesan, egg, and herbs in a bowl. Mix well and season with salt and pepper. Spoon the filling into a pastry bag fitted with a plain tip and pipe the filling into each blossom. Pinch the tops closed and set aside.

To make the batter, whisk the eggs until blended, then whisk in the flour, salt, and pepper. Slowly add the water or club soda and whisk until smooth. The batter should just coat a wooden spoon. (If made in advance, refrigerate for up to 2 hours, then thin with more water or club soda if necessary.)

To fry the blossoms, pour the oil to a depth of 3 inches into a deep sauté pan or saucepan and heat to 350°F. Holding a blossom by the stem end, gently dip it into the batter. Let the excess batter drain away, then quickly and carefully drop the blossom into the hot oil. Repeat, adding only a few blossoms at a time, as you do not want to crowd them in the pan. Fry, turning gently as necessary, until golden on all sides, about 4 minutes. Using a wire skimmer, transfer to paper towels to drain briefly. Repeat with the remaining blossoms. Sprinkle with coarse salt and serve immediately.

MATCHING POINTER: *Rosé is good with these fried blossoms, plus the blush color provides an attractive visual aesthetic. If you want a white, think Sauvignon Blanc.* ❁ **ITALIAN WINES:** CERASUOLO DI VITTORIA, ROSATO DEI COLLI (FRIULI) ❁ **ALTERNATIVE WINES:** "VIN GRIS" OF PINOT NOIR (FRANCE, CALIFORNIA), ROSÉ (PROVENCE)

Ribollita refritto

BEAN-AND-BREAD SOUP "PANCAKE"

Ribollita *means "reboiled." On the first day, this hearty, winter bean-and-vegetable dish is much like a minestrone. On the second day, it is thickened with stale bread and reheated for a truly rib-sticking soup. Then finally, on the third day, it is so dense that it is sautéed in a pan and turned out onto a plate, much like a frittata. At all three stages, it is anointed with a drizzle of extra-virgin olive oil at the table. The best* ribollita *I have ever eaten was served at Carlo Cioni's restaurant, Da Delfina, in Artemino, near the Tuscan town of Carmignano. While Cioni's establishment is not a wine bar,* ribollita refritto *appears on innumerable enoteca menus as well, such as the Il Cantinone del Gallo Nero and La Cantinetta Antinori, both in Florence. The reasons why are simple: it can be quickly fried to order, and it stands up well to a robust Tuscan red wine. Keep in mind that the two initial soups are quite good as well, so practice restraint if you want to try the so-called pancake.*

Serves 6

½ cup extra-virgin olive oil, plus more for drizzling

2 onions, chopped

4 celery stalks, chopped

3 carrots, peeled and chopped

2 cloves garlic, minced

1 cup drained canned plum tomatoes, chopped

1 to 2 tablespoons tomato paste

1 pound Savoy cabbage or *cavolo nero*, or a mixture of kale, Swiss chard, and
   Savoy cabbage, cored and/or tough stems removed and coarsely chopped or shredded

3 cups cooked cannellini beans (see note)

1 tablespoon chopped fresh thyme

Salt and freshly ground black pepper

About 8 cups water

6 to 8 slices country bread

Olive oil for drizzling

Warm the ½ cup olive oil in a large soup kettle over medium heat. Add the onions, celery, carrots, and garlic and sauté until the onions are soft and translucent, about 10 minutes. Add the tomatoes and the tomato paste to taste and cook, stirring occasionally, for 5 minutes. Add the greens, the cooked white beans and their cooking liquid, the thyme, the salt and pepper to taste, and enough water just to cover the vegetables. Bring to a boil, reduce the heat to low, cover, and simmer until all the vegetables are very tender, about 2 hours. If desired, you can serve the soup now as a kind of minestrone.

To make the *ribollita,* layer the bread slices in a large, heavy soup kettle, alternating them with ladlefuls of the soup. Carefully bring the soup to a slow boil over low heat, stirring often to make sure that the bottom doesn't scorch. Cook, stirring often to break down the bread, until the bread has broken down completely and absorbed the liquid, forming a very thick soup, 15 to 20 minutes. If you like, you can serve some, or all, of this very thick soup at this point. Simply ladle it into bowls and drizzle it with olive oil. Or you can let it cool and thicken even more and then sauté it the next day as a pancake.

To make the pancake, drizzle a little olive oil in a small nonstick pan over medium heat. Drop a ladleful of the bread-thickened *ribollita* into the pan, forming a kind of pancake, and sauté over medium heat, turning once, until lightly browned on both sides, about 8 minutes total. Slide the pancake onto a plate and drizzle with olive oil. Repeat to make more pancakes. Serve hot.

<u>Note</u>: Prepare the white beans as directed for Bean Salad with Shrimp (page 95).

MATCHING POINTER: *This dish is designed for the Sangiovese grape. Select a lighter- to medium-bodied style over a heavily oaked, Cabernet-blended Super Tuscan.* ❁ **ITALIAN WINES:** ROSSO DI MONTALCINO, CHIANTI (SENESE, PISANE, ARETINE) ❁ **ALTERNATIVE WINES:** LIGHTER SYRAH AND GRENACHE RHÔNE BLENDS (FRANCE, CALIFORNIA), SANGIOVESE (CALIFORNIA, ARGENTINA)

Torte salate, focaccia, e crostini
SAVORY PASTRIES AND BREADS

Torta di formaggio e funghi CHEESE AND MUSHROOM TART

Pizza rustica RUSTIC MEAT-AND-CHEESE PIE

Piadena GRIDDLED FLATBREAD FROM ROMAGNA

Focaccia con cipolle, gorgonzola, e noce
ONION, GORGONZOLA, AND WALNUT FOCACCIA

Torta di riso RICE TART

Torta di verdura LIGURIAN GREENS PIE

Crostini di fegatini alla fiorentina CHICKEN LIVER CROSTINI

Crostini di granchio CRAB SALAD ON POLENTA CROSTINI

Schiacciata all'uva HARVEST GRAPE FOCACCIA

Tre crostini A TRIO OF CROSTINI

left: *Schiacciata all'uva*
HARVEST GRAPE FOCACCIA, page 58

Torte salate, focaccia, e crostini
SAVORY PASTRIES AND BREADS

AN ENOTECA would be lost without its assortment of breads. Even if it has no kitchen, *crostini, bruschette,* and sandwiches can be assembled easily, and focaccia and savory pastries can be purchased at a neighboring *gastronomia* or bakery. Delicate single-crusted tarts or heartier double-crusted pies called *torte salate* form a significant segment of the menu. These might be filled simply with cheese and eggs or more elaborately with mushrooms or greens. Another kind of *torta,* called *pizza rustica,* has a hearty filling of eggs and cheese interlaced with pork, sausage, and ham.

It would be a rare enoteca that has space for a wood-burning pizza oven, but owners purchase or make flatbreads earlier in the day and may warm them just before serving. These range from a plain dough sprinkled with coarse salt and sage, to a more complex focaccia scented with rosemary and topped with grapes and walnuts as an accompaniment for a wedge of ripe cheese. *Piadena,* a tortillalike flatbread from Emilia-Romagna, is rolled out paper-thin, quickly cooked on a hot griddle, and then smeared with runny cheese or wrapped around greens or slices of sausage. All pair wonderfully with wine.

Bread is used as a base for many other enoteca foods. The most familiar are *bruschette, crostini,* and *tartine. Bruschetta* is a thick slice of country bread, grilled, brushed with extra-virgin olive oil, and rubbed with garlic. In its simplest, unadorned form, it is called *fettunta,* but many versions are crowned with chopped tomatoes or slices of prosciutto or other popular toppings. *Crostini* are smaller than *bruschette* and the bread is toasted through. They also serve as a vehicle for an endless variety of toppings. The *tartine* is an open-faced sandwich, usually made with a roll or slim loaf halved lengthwise, then layered with sliced meats, cheeses, and the like. Even slices of cooked polenta can be grilled, fried, or warmed in the oven and served as *crostini.* The cornmeal adds sweetness and is a lovely match with sweet shellfish or sausage and cured ham.

In enotecas that lack a full kitchen, the staff is adept at creating *bruschette* and *crostini* in countertop ovens. Here are two favorites from the Enoteca di Cormons in Friuli: grilled bread topped with sautéed mushrooms, covered with mozzarella, and broiled, then served with a glass of Pinot Grigio, and grilled bread topped with diced tomatoes that have been sautéed briefly with basil, garlic, and oil, mixed with diced mozzarella, and put under the broiler until the cheese melts. Other toppings for *crostini* or *bruschette* you might want to try include slices of mozzarella and prosciutto with olive purée, or bread spread with pesto and topped with chopped or sliced tomatoes and mozzarella.

Many of the enotecas like to create signature cheese spreads, some mixed with herbs, others with chopped nuts. Some cover *bruschetta* with sautéed broccoli rabe and melted sheep cheese. Others top grilled or toasted bread with caramelized onions and diced sausage. Still other toppings might include mashed cannellini beans crowned with thin slivers of red onion, chopped salami, or sautéed radicchio or other bitter greens. Other favorites include chopped roasted eggplant with capers and olives, goat cheese and roasted peppers, tuna and anchovies with capers, and chopped tomatoes and arugula.

Bread also makes its appearance on the enoteca countertop in the form of Italian sandwiches known as *panini* and *tramezzini. Panini* are made with small, soft rolls and have simple fillings. Some of them, such as Fontina and prosciutto or Fontina and olive purée, may be grilled on a sandwich press and served hot. Others are offered at room temperature. *Tramezzini* are made with thinly sliced white bread, crusts removed, and are much like tea sandwiches. They may be filled with just butter and a slice of prosciutto or salami, or smoked salmon and a layer of horseradish cream, and are always cut on the diagonal, forming delicate triangles. Other fillings are egg salad with anchovies and capers; salami or *coppa* with herbed cheese; tuna salad with olives, onions, and lemon mayonnaise; ham and celery with mustard mayonnaise; chicken salad with celery, pine nuts, and raisins; and chopped shrimp in a lemon mayonnaise with watercress or arugula. The combinations are infinite and, inevitably, wine worthy.

＊

Torta di formaggio e funghi
CHEESE AND MUSHROOM TART

Perfect with wine, the torta di formaggio *uses* pasta frolla salata, *a short pastry, and a* besciamella-*based filling. At its simplest, it may be prepared with a mixture of grated cheeses, but the Enoteca Baccus in Bolzano adds sautéed mushrooms for a deeper flavor and earthy perfume. Other versions add cooked spinach in place of the mushrooms.*

Serves 6 to 8

PASTRY:

1½ cups all-purpose flour

Pinch of salt

6 tablespoons chilled unsalted butter

1 egg, lightly beaten

About 2 tablespoons ice water

FILLING:

6 tablespoons plus ¼ cup unsalted butter

⅓ cup all-purpose flour

3 cups milk, heated

½ pound fresh porcini mushrooms, sliced (see note)

2 whole eggs, separated, plus 2 egg whites

1¾ cups grated cheese such as Gruyère, Fontina, or *grana,* or a mixture

Salt and freshly ground black pepper

Freshly grated nutmeg

To make the pastry, stir together the flour and salt in a bowl. Cut in the butter with a pastry blender until the mixture resembles coarse meal. Add the egg and enough ice water for the dough to come together into a rough ball. Form into a disk, wrap in plastic wrap, and chill for 1 hour.

Select a 10-inch pie pan or fluted tart pan with a removable bottom or a 9-inch springform pan.

On a lightly floured work surface, roll out the pastry into a 12-inch round about ⅛ inch thick. Carefully transfer the dough round to the pan and ease it into the bottom and sides. Fold the edges under and crimp attractively. Set aside in the refrigerator or freezer until ready to fill and bake.

Preheat the oven to 375°F.

To make the filling, first make a rich cream sauce, or *besciamella*: Melt the 6 tablespoons butter in a saucepan over medium heat. Whisk in the flour and cook, stirring, until it is well incorporated, about 3 minutes. Slowly stir in the hot milk and cook, stirring often, until quite thick and the flour has lost all of its raw taste, about 8 minutes. Remove from the heat and set aside.

Melt the ¼ cup butter in a sauté pan over medium-high heat. Add the mushrooms and sauté until tender and the liquid evaporates, 8 to 10 minutes. Remove from the heat, transfer to a cutting board, and chop coarsely. Set aside.

In a small bowl, beat the egg yolks until blended, then fold into the cream sauce along with the cheese and the mushrooms. Season with salt, pepper, and nutmeg. In another bowl, beat the egg whites until stiff peaks form. Fold the egg whites into the cheese mixture. Pour into the prepared pastry shell.

Bake the tart until golden, 25 to 30 minutes. Transfer to a rack to cool for 10 to 15 minutes. Remove the pan sides and slide the tart onto a serving plate, or leave in the pie pan. Serve warm or at room temperature.

Note: Fresh porcini are traditionally used, but you can substitute cultivated mushrooms for them. To give these blander mushrooms a bigger flavor, soak a small handful of dried porcini mushrooms (about ½ ounce) in hot water to soften. After 30 minutes, drain them, reserving the soaking liquid, chop coarsely, and add to the pan with the fresh mushrooms. Strain the soaking liquid through a cheesecloth-lined sieve and add to the eggs.

MATCHING POINTER: *The mushrooms (especially fragrant and earthy porcini) steer this dish to a red. Don't overpower it with too muscular a wine, but nothing too light will stand up to it either.* ❋ **ITALIAN WINES:** NEBBIOLO D'ALBA, MONTEPULCIANO D'ABRUZZO ❋ **ALTERNATIVE WINES:** RIOJA OR SIMILAR SPANISH TEMPRANILLO WINE, LIGHT-OAK-AGED MERLOT FROM ANYWHERE

※

Pizza Rustica

RUSTIC MEAT-AND-CHEESE PIE

This pie is rich and filling, so you don't need to eat much of it. A small slice is the perfect foil for a glass of red wine. The sweet crust is typical of the Abruzzo. Pizza rustica is also popular in and around Campania, and therefore with the Italo-American community of southern Italian descent living on the East Coast of the United States.

<u>Serves 12</u>

PASTRY:

2½ cups all-purpose flour

¼ cup sugar

2 teaspoons baking powder

½ teaspoon salt

½ cup chilled unsalted butter

2 eggs, lightly beaten

About 4 tablespoons ice water

FILLING:

2 tablespoons olive oil

½ pound sweet Italian sausages

½ pound lean pork, cut into ½-inch cubes

¼ pound mortadella, diced (optional)

4 cups (about 2 pounds) ricotta cheese

½ pound fresh mozzarella cheese, cut into ½-inch cubes

½ pound provolone cheese, cut into ½-inch cubes

½ cup grated Parmesan cheese

6 eggs, lightly beaten

¼ cup chopped fresh flat-leaf parsley

Salt and freshly ground black pepper

Pinch of ground cinnamon or freshly grated nutmeg (optional)

Lightly beaten egg for brushing

To make the pastry, stir together the flour, sugar, baking powder, and salt in a bowl. Cut in the butter until the mixture resembles coarse meal. Add the eggs and enough ice water for the dough to come together in a rough ball. Form into 2 disks, one slightly larger than the other. Wrap in plastic wrap and chill for 1 hour.

Meanwhile, make the filling: Warm the olive oil in a sauté pan over medium heat. Add the sausages and fry until cooked through, about 8 minutes. Remove from the heat and, when cool enough to handle, remove the casings and crumble or cut into small pieces. Place in a bowl. Fry the pork cubes in the same pan over medium heat until cooked through and golden but not dry, about 8 minutes. Add to the bowl. Then add the mortadella (if using), ricotta, mozzarella, provolone, Parmesan, eggs, and parsley to the meats and mix well. Season with salt, pepper, and the cinnamon or nutmeg, if using.

Preheat the oven to 400°F.

On a lightly floured surface, roll out the larger disk into a 14-inch round about ¼ inch thick. Carefully transfer the dough round to a 10-inch springform pan and ease it into the bottom and sides. Trim the overhang to about ½ inch and flatten it to make a rim. Spoon the filling into the crust. Roll out the remaining disk into a 10-inch round about ⅛ inch thick. Moisten the edges of the bottom crust with water. Carefully transfer the dough round to the pan, placing it over the filling. Securely pinch the edges of the top and bottom crusts together. Cut a few steam vents in the surface, and brush the top with the beaten egg.

Bake the pie until the crust is golden, about 1 hour. Transfer to a rack to cool. Remove the pan sides and slide the pie onto a serving platter. Serve at room temperature.

MATCHING POINTER: A fuller red wine is in order here. While too much oak is a distraction, ample extraction flavor (such as what one would find in the well-made reds of the Abruzzo) is required. Something a bit more rustic is preferred. ✳ **ITALIAN WINES:** MONTEPULCIANO D'ABRUZZO, NON-RISERVA TAURASI ✳ **ALTERNATIVE WINES:** MEDIUM-BODIED ZINFANDEL (CALIFORNIA), LIGHTER PETITE SIRAH (CALIFORNIA)

Piadena
GRIDDLED FLATBREAD FROM ROMAGNA

Piadena *is peasant food gone fashionable. At one time this rustic flatbread
from Romagna was cooked on an unglazed terra-cotta stone called a* testo. *Today everyone
seems to use a cast-iron griddle. The dough can be prepared ahead of time and
refrigerated, as you might do with pizza dough. It is then rolled out, slapped onto a hot
griddle, and cooked briefly on both sides until speckled golden brown. While it is still
hot, it is folded around slices of salami or prosciutto, a clump of cooked greens, or, as
is the case at Ravenna's Enoteca Bastioni and Enoteca Ca de Ven, spread with* stracchino
cheese or the slightly sour and soupy squaquerone *cheese, another regional specialty.*

The texture of a piadena *resembles that of a flour tortilla. In the past it was
made with lard, and purists still insist that lard is essential. Today it is more often made
with olive oil and milk and a bit of baking powder to make it softer and thus
easier to fold over slices of prosciutto and cheese. This is fast food at its best.*

3 cups all-purpose flour

1 teaspoon salt

½ teaspoon baking powder

3 tablespoons extra-virgin olive oil, or 3 tablespoons chilled lard, cut into small pieces

About ¼ cup each water and milk, or ½ cup water or soda water

Stir together the flour, salt, and baking powder in a bowl. Make a well in the center and add the olive oil or lard and some of the liquid. Mix with a fork, gradually adding all of the liquid—and a bit more if needed—until the dough comes together and leaves the sides of the bowl clean. Turn out onto a lightly floured surface and knead until smooth, about 10 minutes. Form into 6 balls. (You can cover and refrigerate the dough at this point for up to 3 hours before continuing.)

To serve, heat a cast-iron griddle over medium-high heat until a drop of water sizzles and jumps across the surface. While the griddle is heating, roll out the balls of dough on a floured work surface into rounds about ⅛ inch thick. Place a round on the hot griddle, press down with a wide spatula, and leave for 30 seconds. Turn the round over, press down again, and leave for about 30 seconds more. It should be dotted with golden brown specks on both sides. Slow cooking makes the bread too stiff, while fast cooking produces the best and most tender results. Remove from the griddle and repeat with the remaining rounds.

You may keep these breads warm, wrapped in aluminum foil, in a 200°F oven for up to 20 minutes, but like any griddled flatbread, they are best eaten as soon as possible.

Serve hot, wrapped in a napkin, with the fillings of your choice.

MATCHING POINTER: *The flatbread is only a delivery mechanism for transporting your choice of fillings to your mouth. Presuming something "meat" (prosciutto), a simply quaffable red will do; if cheese, choose red or a zippy, young white.* ✳ **ITALIAN WINES:** CHIANTI, DOLCETTO D'ALBA, PINOT GRIGIO ✳ **ALTERNATIVE WINES:** SPANISH OR PORTUGUESE SIMPLER REDS, JUICY, SIMPLE SHIRAZ (AUSTRALIA)

✳

Focaccia con cipolle, gorgonzola, e noce

ONION, GORGONZOLA, AND WALNUT FOCACCIA

When you sit down at one of the few tables at the Osteria da Cencio in the town of Cento, near Ferrara, the host will bring you the cestino del fornaio, *a basket with the breads and focaccia of the day. The osteria has been in operation since 1850, carries over a hundred wines, and specializes in foods of the region. Although the Gorgonzola is a touch of Lombardy, the sweet caramelized onions are much enjoyed in the Veneto. The addition of mildly bitter walnuts and tart and creamy Gorgonzola harmonizes so beautifully with wine that this focaccia is a wine bar staple. You can bake it ahead of time and warm it just slightly before serving. It's also good at room temperature, as it is not too cheesy.*

Serves 8

Dough for Harvest Grape Focaccia (page 58), made with ⅓ cup buckwheat flour in place of ⅓ cup of the all-purpose flour (optional) and 3 tablespoons chopped fresh rosemary or sage (optional)

TOPPING:
¼ cup unsalted butter
3 pounds red onions (about 3 large), sliced about ¼ inch thick
Salt and freshly ground black pepper
1 cup (5 ounces) crumbled Gorgonzola *dolcelatte* cheese
½ cup walnuts, toasted and chopped
Olive oil for brushing

Make the dough as directed through the second rising, adding the buckwheat flour and rosemary or sage, if desired.

While the dough is rising, make the topping: Melt the butter in a heavy, wide sauté pan over low heat. Add the onions and cook slowly, stirring occasionally, until quite soft, golden brown, and reduced, about 30 minutes. Season with salt and pepper and remove from the heat. If the onions seem too soupy, drain in a sieve.

Preheat the oven to 475°F.

To top the dough, dimple the surface with your fingers at regular intervals, forming shallow indentations. Spread the cooled onions evenly on top, then distribute little chunks of the Gorgonzola over the onions and sprinkle with the walnuts.

Bake until the crust is puffed and golden and the walnuts are browned and crisp, about 12 minutes. Remove from the oven and brush the edges of the crust lightly with olive oil. Serve warm or at room temperature, cut into squares.

MATCHING POINTER: *This savory treatment rides the wave of sweet (caramelized onions), salty, (Gorgonzola), and a hint of bitter (walnuts). Red wine leaves a metallic off-taste, so stay white or off-dry rosé.* ❋ **ITALIAN WINES:** MOSCATO D'ASTI, ROSATO DI SAN GIMIGNANO ❋ **ALTERNATIVE WINES:** WHITE ZINFANDEL, OFF-DRY RIESLING (GERMANY, ALSACE, AUSTRIA)

❋

Torta di riso
RICE TART

Torta *is the Italian word for "cake," but it can also refer to a savory pie, or* torta salata. Torte salate *are found all over Italy, but they are a particular specialty of Liguria and Emilia-Romagna. A* torta *may have a single bottom crust with the sides of the crust flipped over and partially covering the filling, much like a* galette, *or they may have a top and a bottom crust. Although traditionally round and typically baked in springform pans for ease of serving,* torte *are sometimes baked in large rectangular pans and cut into squares when volume is a consideration.* Torte *are best served warm or at room temperature.*

The pastry dough given here is quite elastic and lean; but for holidays, cooks sometimes make a richer pasta frolla salata *(double the pastry recipe for the Cheese and Mushroom Tart, page 42). A* torta *can also be baked in a buttered baking dish without a crust. It is then called a* tortino. *Many recipes were sent to me by Pino Sola of Enoteca Sola, in Genoa, and this one is from his book* Ricette e vini di Liguria. *Sola says that the* torta *is delicate and lightly perfumed with garlic and marjoram, which plays off the sweetness of the rice and the earthiness of the mushrooms. Pigato, a Ligurian white wine from Albenga, would be his choice.*

PASTRY:

4 cups all-purpose flour

2 teaspoons salt

¼ cup olive oil

About ¾ cup water, or 6 tablespoons each water and dry white wine

FILLING:

1 cup Carnaroli or other short-grain Italian rice

2 cups milk

4 tablespoons extra-virgin olive oil

1 onion, chopped

2 cloves garlic, minced

1 tablespoon chopped fresh marjoram

½ pound Swiss chard or beet greens, stems removed and finely chopped

4 eggs, lightly beaten

1 scant cup (7 ounces) ricotta or _prescinseua_ cheese (see note)

Small handful (about ½ ounce) dried porcini mushrooms, soaked in hot water
   to soften for 30 minutes, drained, and chopped (optional)

Salt and freshly ground black pepper

Freshly grated nutmeg (optional)

To make the pastry, stir together the flour and salt in a bowl. Add the oil and enough water, or water and wine, for the dough to come together in a rough ball. Form into 2 disks, one slightly larger than the other. Cover with plastic wrap and let rest at room temperature for at least 30 minutes.

Meanwhile, make the filling: Combine the rice and milk in a saucepan, bring to a gentle boil over medium-high heat, cover, reduce to low heat, and cook until the rice is tender, about 15 minutes.

While the rice is cooking, warm 2 tablespoons of the olive oil in a sauté pan over medium heat. Add the onion, garlic, and marjoram and sauté until golden, 12 to 15 minutes. In another sauté pan, warm 1 tablespoon oil and sauté the greens just until wilted, 2 to 3 minutes. Drain well and squeeze out any moisture.

Transfer the rice to a large bowl and stir in the eggs, cheese, onion mixture, the greens, and the porcini, if using. Season with salt, pepper, and the nutmeg, if using. Place in the refrigerator for 10 minutes to cool.

Preheat the oven to 400°F.

On a lightly floured work surface, roll out the larger pastry disk into a 14-inch round about ¼ inch thick. Carefully transfer the dough round to a well-oiled 10-inch springform pan and ease it into the bottom and sides. Trim the overhang to about ½ inch and flatten it to make a rim.

Spoon the cooled rice mixture into the prepared crust. Roll out the remaining pastry disk into a 10-inch round about ¼ inch thick. Moisten the edges of the bottom crust with water. Carefully transfer the dough round to the pan, placing it over the filling. Securely pinch the edges of the top and bottom crusts together. Cut a few steam vents in the surface, and brush the top with the remaining 1 tablespoon oil.

Bake the tart until the filling is set (test with a knife blade inserted through a steam vent) and the crust is golden, 30 to 40 minutes. Transfer to a rack to cool. Remove the pan sides and slide the tart onto a serving plate. Serve warm or at room temperature.

Note: _Prescinseua_ is a staple in the Ligurian kitchen. It resembles curds of clotted cream or clabbered milk. To reproduce its tangy quality, Fred Plotkin, author of the superb _Recipes from Paradise,_ on the food of Liguria, suggests combining equal parts ricotta and plain yogurt or buttermilk.

MATCHING POINTERS: _A blank canvas, wine-wise. While the chard, herbs, and porcini steer one to red, again light is the rule. A full-flavored white wine could be quite nice, as could a robust rosé-styled wine._ ✴ **ITALIAN WINES:** VALTELLINA, BARBERA D'ASTI ✴ **ALTERNATIVE WINES:** TAVEL OR SIMILAR RICH RHÔNE-STYLE ROSÉ, CRU BEAUJOLAIS (FRANCE), NAPA GAMAY (CALIFORNIA)

※

Torta di verdura

LIGURIAN GREENS PIE

The famed greens pie of Liguria is one of the region's signature dishes.
A similar filling is used for torta pasqualina, *the multilayered pie served at Easter,*
but without the pine nuts and raisins and with the addition of cooked artichokes.
In Emilia-Romagna, the greens pie, called erbazzone, *may have some pancetta added.*

<u>Serves 8</u>

Pastry for Rice Tart (page 49)

FILLING:

Olive oil for sautéing

1 onion, chopped

1 bunch fresh flat-leaf parsley, chopped (about ⅓ cup)

6 cups coarsely chopped beet greens, chard, or spinach (2½ to 3 pounds before trimming stems)

2 teaspoons salt

½ teaspoon freshly ground black pepper

½ teaspoon freshly grated nutmeg, or to taste

¼ cup golden raisins, plumped in hot water and drained

¼ cup pine nuts, toasted

3 eggs, lightly beaten

1 cup (about 8 ounces) ricotta cheese

⅔ cup grated Parmesan cheese

Olive oil or lightly beaten egg for brushing

Make the pastry, divide into 2 disks, cover, and let rest as directed.

To make the filling, pour enough olive oil into a large sauté pan to film the bottom. Add the onion and parsley and sauté over medium heat until the onion softens, 3 to 4 minutes. Add the greens, stir until wilted, cover, reduce heat to low, and cook slowly until the mixture is almost dry, 10 to 15 minutes.

Remove from the heat, drain well, and season with the salt, pepper, and nutmeg. Stir in the raisins and pine nuts. Let cool, then fold in the eggs and cheeses.

Preheat the oven to 375°F.

On a lightly floured work surface, roll out the larger pastry disk into a 14-inch round about ¼ inch thick. Carefully transfer the dough round to a 10-inch springform pan and ease it into the bottom and sides. Trim the overhang to about ½ inch and flatten it to make a rim. Spoon the greens mixture into the prepared crust. Roll out the remaining pastry disk into a 10-inch round about a ¼ inch thick. Moisten the edges of the bottom crust with water. Carefully transfer the dough round to the pan, placing it over the filling. Securely pinch the edges of the top and bottom crusts together. Cut a few steam vents in the surface, and brush the top with olive oil or beaten egg.

Bake the pie until the crust is golden, about 40 minutes. Transfer to a rack to cool. Remove the pan sides and slide the tart onto a serving plate. Serve warm or at room temperature.

Note: If you are worried about the bottom crust becoming soggy because of the moisture in the greens, sprinkle a thin layer of fine dried bread crumbs over the pastry before adding the filling. Alternatively, line the crust with aluminum foil and pie weights and partially bake it in a 400°F oven for 15 minutes. Let cool before adding the filling.

MATCHING POINTER: _Rich and full flavored from the greens, yet with a sweet edge from the pine nuts and raisins, the preparation is best with a muscular white or one with ample personality (if lighter in body). A lightly herbal red would also be good._ ✳ **ITALIAN WINES:** TOCAI FRIULANO, VERDUZZO FRIULANO, CHARDONNAY (FRIULI, LANGHE) ✳ **ALTERNATIVE WINES:** SAUVIGNON BLANC (NEW ZEALAND), WHITE RHÔNE BLENDS (FRANCE, CALIFORNIA)

※

Crostini di fegatini alla fiorentina
CHICKEN LIVER CROSTINI

Enoteca Bar Fuori Porta, in Florence, is known for its wide assortment of
crostini and bruschette. This Florentine classic is one of many offered as a nibble to start
a meal along with a glass of the local Chianti. It can be prepared a few hours ahead of time
and kept at room temperature, or the spread can be made the day before and warmed at serving
time. Some versions of this recipe use lemon juice or lemon zest in place of the capers,
but be careful not to let the mixture get too tart, or it will fight with the wine.
Others use a bit of anchovy. Just be careful not to overcook the livers. They need to be
creamy and moist for this spread to hold up well.

Makes about 24

4 tablespoons unsalted butter

4 tablespoons olive oil

1½ cups chopped onion

6 to 8 fresh sage leaves

1 pound chicken livers, well trimmed

½ cup dry white wine

2 to 3 tablespoons finely chopped rinsed capers (optional)

Salt and freshly ground black pepper

12 thick slices coarse country bread, halved and toasted or grilled

Chopped fresh flat-leaf parsley for garnish

Melt 2 tablespoons each of the butter and olive oil in a large sauté pan over medium heat. Add the onion and sage leaves and sauté until the onion is soft and translucent, 8 to 10 minutes. Melt the remaining 2 tablespoons each butter and olive oil in another sauté pan over medium heat. Add the livers and fry quickly, turning often, until cooked through but still very pink in the middle, no more than 5 minutes. Add the onion mixture and the wine to the livers and cook for 1 or 2 minutes longer to blend the flavors.

Transfer half of the liver mixture to a food processor and pulse briefly to form a coarse purée. Do not overprocess, as you want some texture. Transfer to a bowl. Repeat with the remaining liver mixture and transfer to the bowl. Stir in any remaining pan juices and the capers, if using. Season with salt and pepper.

Spread the chicken liver purée on the bread and sprinkle with a little chopped parsley. Serve warm or at room temperature.

MATCHING POINTER: *The pungent personality of chicken livers can break up wines and make them taste sour. Err on the side of overpowering them, which leaves some room for the chicken livers to "take away" something from the wine.* ✳ **ITALIAN WINES:** CARMIGNANO, ROSSO DI MONTALCINO ✳ **ALTERNATIVE WINES:** CÔTES DU RHÔNE, LIGHT- TO MEDIUM-BODIED CABERNET SAUVIGNON

✳

Crostini di granchio
CRAB SALAD ON POLENTA CROSTINI

Seafood crostini are most often served in Friuli and the Veneto, but other enoteca proprietors know a good thing when they taste it, so shellfish-topped crostini appear on wine bar menus from north to south, from I Vini di Mariu's in Milan to the Enoteca Perrazzo on Ischia, in the Bay of Naples. Other delicious seafood toppings include chopped steamed clams tossed with olive oil, lemon, pine nuts, and parsley, or a mixture of crabmeat scented with orange zest and mixed with minced green onions or chopped arugula and olive oil.

Serves 8

2 tablespoons olive oil
1 small onion, minced
½ cup finely diced celery
1 pound crabmeat, picked over for shell fragments and cartilage
Grated zest of 1 lemon
2 tablespoons fresh lemon juice
3 tablespoons chopped fresh chives
3 tablespoons chopped fresh flat-leaf parsley, plus more for garnish (optional)
1 tablespoon Dijon mustard

½ cup mayonnaise, or as needed
Salt and freshly ground black pepper
¼ teaspoon cayenne pepper, or to taste
Polenta *crostini* (page 102)

Warm the olive oil in a small sauté pan over medium heat. Add the onion and celery and sauté until soft and sweet, 8 to 10 minutes. Transfer to a bowl and let cool.

Add the crab, lemon zest and juice, chives, 3 tablespoons parsley, and the mustard to the onion mixture, mix well, and then add enough of the mayonnaise to bind the mixture. Season with salt, black pepper, and cayenne pepper. Cover and chill well.

Spread the crab mixture on the warm *crostini*. Top with additional chopped parsley, if desired. Serve at once.

MATCHING POINTER: *A perfect dish to show off rich and aromatic white wines. It lends itself beautifully to the wines of its locale (Friuli), but it can venture to wherever velvety, smooth whites of character and texture flourish.* ✳ **ITALIAN WINES:** CHARDONNAY BLENDS (FRIULI), GRECO DI TUFO ✳ **ALTERNATIVE WINES:** LIGHT-OAK-AGED CHARDONNAY, SÉMILLON BLENDS (AUSTRALIA, WASHINGTON STATE)

✻

Schiacciata all'uva

HARVEST GRAPE FOCACCIA

If you are looking for a perfect flatbread to pair with cheese, this could be it.
A grape harvest specialty all over Tuscany, the seasoned bread carries some sweetness from
the grapes to contrast with creamy cheeses such as robiola, caprino, *or* ricotta. *This* schiacciata
is served at L'Enoteca in Carrara Marina, the port of the famous Tuscan marble town.

<u>Serves 8</u>

SPONGE:

2 teaspoons active dry yeast

½ cup warm water

2 tablespoons sugar

½ cup all-purpose flour

DOUGH:

¾ cup water

3 tablespoons walnut oil

1 teaspoon salt

3⅓ cups all-purpose flour

1 tablespoon chopped fresh rosemary (optional)

TOPPING:

Walnut oil for brushing

1 cup coarsely chopped toasted walnuts or hazelnuts

2 cups seedless red grapes, halved lengthwise

¼ cup sugar

To make the sponge, sprinkle the yeast over the warm water in a large bowl and let stand until foamy, about 10 minutes. Add the sugar and flour and stir to combine. Cover and let stand at room temperature until bubbly, about 30 minutes.

To make the dough, add the water, walnut oil, salt, flour, and the rosemary, if using, to the sponge and stir until the dough comes together. Turn out onto a floured work surface and knead until soft and smooth, about 10 minutes. (Or knead in a stand mixer with a dough hook on low speed.) Form into a ball, place in an oiled bowl, cover the bowl with a towel, and let the dough rise in a warm place until doubled in bulk, about 1 hour.

Turn the dough out onto a lightly floured work surface, punch down, and form into an 11-by-18-inch rectangle. Transfer to an oiled baking sheet. Cover the dough with a towel and let rise until doubled in bulk, 15 to 30 minutes.

Preheat the oven to 400°F.

To top the dough, brush it with a little walnut oil and dimple the surface with your fingers at regular intervals, forming shallow indentations. Top with the nuts and grapes, pushing the grape halves into the dough and spacing them evenly. Sprinkle them with the sugar.

Bake until golden and the sugar is slightly caramelized, 12 to 15 minutes. Serve warm or at room temperature, cut into squares.

MATCHING POINTER: Great possibilities exist here, as playing the sweet-salt dynamic is always interesting. Don't overlook fizz, as it is apropos in this case. Otherwise, go with a kiss of sweetness in a sharper-styled wine. ✳ **ITALIAN WINES:** PROSECCO, MOSCATO GIALLO (FRIULI) ✳ **ALTERNATIVE WINES:** RUSTIC, OFF-DRY CHENIN BLANC (VOUVRAY), SPARKLING WINE (LOIRE VALLEY, CALIFORNIA, AUSTRALIA)

※

Tre crostini
A TRIO OF CROSTINI

Here are three other quick-and-easy crostini *toppings that can be made in a food processor.*

<u>*Puré di tonno*/Tuna Purée</u>: Combine 7 ounces drained canned tuna and 6 to 8 tablespoons room-temperature unsalted butter in a food processor. Process until smooth. Season with a little fresh lemon juice, salt, and freshly ground black pepper. Top with capers and parsley. Serve with a glass of Bianco di Custoza, Bianco di Pitigliano, Pinot Grigio, Sauvignon Blanc, or Pinot Blanc.

<u>*Puré di gorgonzola e nocciole*/Gorgonzola and Hazelnut Purée</u>: Combine 2 parts Gorgonzola cheese and 1 part room-temperature unsalted butter in a food processor. Process until smooth. Fold in chopped, toasted hazelnuts. Top with a thin slice of ripe pear or fig, if desired, or with chopped fennel or celery. Serve with a glass of Arneis, Chardonnay (Alto Adige), unoaked Chardonnay, or dry Riesling.

<u>*Puré di fagioli*/White Bean Purée</u>: Combine 2 cups drained cooked white beans, ½ cup extra-virgin olive oil, and 2 or 3 garlic cloves, chopped, in a food processor. Process until smooth. Season with salt and freshly ground black pepper. Top with a bit of chopped wilted bitter greens or diced salami. Serve with a glass of Albana di Romagna, Sauvignon (Friuli), Pinot Gris/Grigio (United States), or Sauvignon Blanc (Chile).

Pasta al forno
PASTAS AND GRAINS

Pasta all'uovo **BASIC EGG PASTA**

Tre salse per pasta **THREE SAUCES FOR PASTA**

Rotoli di pasta **STUFFED PASTA ROLLS**

Ripieni per pasta **FILLINGS FOR PASTA**

Cannelloni **STUFFED PASTA TUBES**

Pasta al forno alla bolognese
OVEN-BAKED PASTA WITH CLASSIC BOLOGNESE SAUCE

Pasta al cartoccio con gamberi e peperoni rossi
PASTA PACKETS WITH SHRIMP AND SWEET RED PEPPERS

Maccheroni al porro, salsicce, e porcini
PASTA GRATIN WITH LEEKS, SAUSAGES, AND MUSHROOMS

Risotto al salto **RISOTTO PANCAKE**

Bomba di riso
**BAKED RICE CASSEROLE FILLED WITH SAUSAGE
AND CHEESE**

left: *Pasta al cartoccio con gamberi e peperoni rossi*
PASTA PACKETS WITH SHRIMP AND SWEET RED PEPPERS, page 78

Pasta al forno
PASTAS AND GRAINS

TO COOK PASTA that meets the high standards of the Italian palate requires an experienced kitchen staff, sufficient burners on the stove, and the time to turn out preparations to order. These conditions eliminate pasta from the menus of many enotecas. Only those with a full kitchen or attached to an *osteria* or *ristorante* can pass the test.

The enoteca does not have to ignore pasta altogether, however. Lasagna, cannelloni, or filled pasta rolls that may be fully assembled and completely cooked in advance are intelligent options for the average wine bar. Individual portions can be reheated in the oven or microwave in a matter of minutes. *Pasta al forno,* tossed with sauce and spooned into ramekins, or *al cartoccio,* enclosed in foil or paper packets, are practical choices, too. The classic *ragù alla bolognese,* a rich meat sauce, and *besciamella,* the basic cream sauce, can do double duty as sauces for *pasta al forno*

or a hearty lasagna. Tomato sauce is a multipurpose player in the pasta kitchen, too.

With its equally demanding timing requirements, risotto is also impractical for most enoteca staffs to execute. *Risotto al salto,* a sautéed risotto pancake, or *bomba di riso,* a filled timbale of baked rice, do fit the wine bar format, however. Individual portions of these quick-and-easy dishes can be reheated in the oven or microwave, with or without sauce.

Polenta is a good candidate for the enoteca menu as well. *Polenta pastizzada,* sliced cooked polenta layered with *ragù alla bolognese* and topped with grated Parmesan, is easy to assemble and reheats nicely. Polenta slices can also be put in a gratin dish, drizzled with melted butter, sprinkled with grated cheese, and heated. A rich *fonduta* (page 168) or a mushroom sauce (page 146) spooned over sliced polenta is an equally satisfying dish.

Whether bought fresh at a pasta shop or picked up from the freezer case, gnocchi are convenient for the enoteca or home cook. When potato gnocchi have been parboiled and carefully covered mixed with a sauce, they can be held for an hour or two in a gratin dish and reheated successfully in the oven. Drizzle them with melted butter and sprinkle with grated Parmesan for the simplest dish, or opt for a richer version such as *gnocchi alla bolognese* with a rich meat sauce, *gnocchi alla salsa di gorgonzola* with a light *besciamella* topped with crumbled Gorgonzola, or *gnocchi alla fonduta piemontese* with truffle oil (page 168). You can also dress the gnocchi with melted butter, chopped tomatoes or a light tomato sauce, and cooked seafood such as crab or shrimp, and again slip the dish into the oven. Here, as elsewhere, the key to serving pasta and other grain-based dishes in the enoteca is *al forno*—"baked in the oven."

Pasta all'uovo

BASIC EGG PASTA

It is easy to buy fresh pasta nowadays, although most prepackaged supermarket pasta is rarely as delicate and tender as the pasta you can make at home. To make your own, all you need is a small hand-cranked pasta machine. (Please don't use an electric-type extruder, which produces an elastic and often tough dough.)

The following recipe makes a rather stiff dough that ultimately yields a nice, light pasta. A drier dough produces pasta that does not become gummy when cooked, so take the time to knead this somewhat resistant dough and you will be rewarded with silky noodles.

Use unbleached all-purpose flour, not the coarser semolina flour, for a tender noodle. To measure it, spoon it into a measuring cup and then level it with a knife. Weather affects pasta, so if the day is damp, you may need a bit less flour. For the richest pasta, use more egg yolks than whole eggs, following the formula of 3 egg yolks is equal to 1 whole egg. Italians make gorgeous fresh pasta with deep orange egg yolks called rosso d'uovo, *"the red of the egg." Some cooks even pride themselves on the number of egg yolks they can incorporate into the dough. If you want to join them, substitute a dozen yolks for the whole eggs in the following recipe.*

<u>Makes about 1½ pounds, enough for 8 small first-course servings or 6 main-course portions</u>

3 to 3¼ cups unbleached all-purpose flour

1 teaspoon salt

4 whole eggs, or 3 whole large and 3 egg yolks, lightly beaten

3 to 4 tablespoons water, or as needed

To make the dough by hand, stir together 3 cups flour and the salt in a large bowl. Make a well in the center and add the whole eggs or whole eggs and eggs yolks. With a fork, gradually pull the flour into the well until all of it is incorporated and a supple dough has formed. If it seems too dry, add a bit of the water. If it is too wet, add a bit more flour. Turn the dough out onto a lightly floured work surface and knead until the dough is smooth, 10 to 15 minutes. (If you don't feel like kneading the dough by hand, you may knead it in an electric stand mixer fitted with a dough hook.) Divide the dough in half and pat into 2 flattened disks. Slip the disks into a plastic bag and allow the dough to rest at room temperature for 30 to 60 minutes, to give the gluten in the flour time to relax.

Alternatively, make the pasta dough in a food processor: Put the 3 cups flour and the salt in a processor and pulse briefly to mix. Add the whole eggs or whole eggs and yolks and pulse, adding a bit of water if needed, or more flour, until the dough comes together in a rough ball. (Resist the temptation to add too much water, or the dough will be too soft and sticky to roll out after it rests.) Gather the dough into a ball (it will be crumbly) and place on a lightly floured surface. Knead until smooth, 10 to 15 minutes. Form into 2 disks and let rest as directed in hand method.

When you are ready to roll out the pasta, divide each disk into 2 or 3 pieces. Work with one piece at a time, keeping the others in the plastic bag to prevent them from drying out. Flatten each piece into a rectangle about the width of the rollers of a hand-cranked pasta machine. It should be thin enough to fit through the widest setting of the machine. Set the rollers at the widest setting, then roll the dough through the rollers. Fold the dough into thirds and roll it through two more times. Fold it in thirds again and roll it through one more time. Now proceed to roll it through each succeeding setting on the machine, making it thinner with each pass until you have rolled it through the narrowest setting.

For lasagna: Roll out the dough through the narrowest setting on the machine as directed. With a pastry wheel, cut into long 3-inch-wide strips to match the dimensions of your lasagna pan with some overlap. To prevent sticking, toss the noodles with a granular flour like fine semolina or cornmeal, place on baking sheets, and cover loosely with plastic wrap or a large plastic bag until you are ready to cook them. To cook, bring a large pot of salted water to a boil, add the pasta, and cook until nearly al dente, about 3 minutes. Drain, rinse with cold water, and lay the strips flat on clean dish towels until needed.

For cannelloni: Roll out the dough through the narrowest setting on the machine as directed. With a pastry wheel, cut into pieces about 4 inches square or 4 by 5 inches. To prevent sticking, toss the pieces with flour or cornmeal and keep as directed for lasagna noodles. Then cook as directed for lasagna noodles, drain, and lay the pieces on clean dish towels until needed. You should have 16 squares or rectangles.

※

Tre salse per pasta

THREE SAUCES FOR PASTA

Tomato sauce is ubiquitous in the Italian kitchen. It may be used for lasagna, to spoon on pasta rolls or cannelloni, or to toss with the pasta of your choice. The olive oil or butter enrichment gives the sauce a smoother finish in the mouth. If the tomatoes are tart, add a pinch of sugar for balance. Both keep for 4 to 5 days in the refrigerator. Besciamella, the classic cream sauce, is a rich enhancement for pasta al forno.

<u>*All sauces make about 3 cups*</u>

※

Salsa di pomodoro ricca

RICH TOMATO SAUCE

3 tablespoons olive oil

1 carrot, peeled and chopped

1 celery stalk, chopped

½ onion, chopped

1 clove garlic, minced

¼ cup chopped fresh flat-leaf parsley

5 large fresh basil leaves, chopped

Salt and freshly ground black pepper to taste

½ cup dry white wine

1 can (28 ounces) plum tomatoes, with their juices, coarsely chopped

Heat the olive oil in a large saucepan over medium heat. Add the carrot, celery, onion, garlic, parsley, and basil and stir well. Season with salt and pepper and sauté until the vegetables are pale gold, about 10 minutes. Add the wine and cook until it evaporates, about 5 minutes. Add the tomatoes with their juices, stir well, reduce the heat to low, and simmer gently, uncovered, until thickened, about 1 hour. Remove from the heat and pass through a food mill if you want a smoother texture.

Salsa di Pomodoro

TOMATO SAUCE

1 can (28 ounces) plum tomatoes, with their juices
½ cup tomato purée
Salt and freshly ground black pepper
2 tablespoons unsalted butter, cut into small pieces (optional)
2 tablespoons extra-virgin olive oil (optional)
Pinch of sugar
6 fresh basil leaves, chopped (optional)
½ cup to ¾ cup heavy cream (optional)

Place the tomatoes and their juices in a food processor and process until finely chopped but not liquefied. Transfer to a heavy saucepan. Stir in the tomato purée and place over low heat. Bring to a simmer and cook, stirring often, until the sauce is slightly thickened, about 20 minutes. Season with salt and pepper. If desired, stir in the butter or olive oil for a smoother finish, and the sugar or basil if needed to balance the flavors. For a richer, sweeter, thinner sauce, stir in the cream.

Salsa besciamella tradizionale

CLASSIC CREAM SAUCE

¼ cup unsalted butter
¼ cup all-purpose flour
2 cups milk or light cream, heated
Salt and freshly ground black pepper
Freshly grated nutmeg

Melt the butter in a saucepan over medium heat. Add the flour and cook, stirring, until it is well incorporated, about 3 minutes. Slowly stir in the hot milk or cream and cook, stirring often, until quite thick and the flour has lost all of its raw taste, about 8 minutes. Season with salt, pepper, and nutmeg and remove from the heat.

Rotoli di pasta
STUFFED PASTA ROLLS

Pasta rolls, or rotoli, *are a specialty of Emilia-Romagna, but, of course, good*
food ideas travel. Rotoli *are featured on the menu at the Circolo Enogastronomico*
per Bacco in Padua, in the neighboring region of the Veneto. The uncooked dough
is spread with a filling, rolled, wrapped, and simmered in salted water. (A fish
poacher or large roasting pan with a rack is ideal.) Once removed and unwrapped,
the rolls can be sliced and served warm as is with a light sauce, or sliced
and placed in a baking dish, topped with melted butter and Parmesan
cheese or a light sauce, and warmed in the oven.

Makes 2; Serves 8 as main-course servings or 16 as appetizer portions

To shape, cook, and serve pasta rolls: Make the Basic Egg Pasta dough (page 66),
divide into 2 disks, and let rest as directed. Make one of the pasta fillings on pages
72-74. On a lightly floured board, roll out 1 disk into a 10-by-20-inch rectangle.
Spread with half of the filling. Starting on a short side, roll up the pasta sheet to
enclose the filling fully. Wrap in cheesecloth or plastic wrap and tie both ends and
then once in the middle with kitchen string. Repeat with the remaining dough disk
and filling. (You may refrigerate the filled dough at this time for up to 2 hours.)

To cook the rolls, bring a wide saucepan filled with salted water to a steady simmer.
Carefully lower the rolls into the water, cover, and simmer for 20 minutes. Remove
carefully from the water and drain well.

Allow the pasta rolls to cool completely, then unwrap. Preheat the oven to 450°F.
Slice the rolls crosswise ½ to 1 inch thick. Arrange the slices in a single layer in a
buttered baking dish. Drizzle lightly with melted butter and sprinkle with grated
Parmesan cheese. Cover the dish with aluminum foil and bake until heated through,
10 to 15 minutes. Serve with a tomato sauce (page 69), if desired.

※

Ripieni per pasta

FILLINGS FOR PASTA

Any one of this trio of fillings goes together quickly and easily.
The pasta rolls and cannelloni can be stuffed and refrigerated for up to 24 hours before cooking.

※

Ripieno ai frutti di mare

SEAFOOD FILLING

4 cups cooked seafood such as chopped shrimp, scallops, or lobster or flaked crabmeat

2 cups not-too-thick cream sauce (page 69)

2 tablespoons chopped fresh flat-leaf parsley

2 tablespoons chopped fresh chives

1 tablespoon grated lemon zest

Salt and freshly ground black pepper

Combine the seafood, cream sauce, parsley, chives, and lemon zest in a bowl and mix well. Taste and season with salt and pepper.

If making pasta rolls, follow the directions for topping and baking included with the general directions. If making cannelloni, follow the directions for shaping and placing in a baking dish, then drizzle with melted unsalted butter, top with a light dusting of bread crumbs or a little tomato sauce (page 69), and heat in the oven as directed.

MATCHING POINTER: *A light-bodied red is fine here, but it is better to opt for a white to highlight the inherent sweetness of the seafood. Some richness is appropriate.* ※ **ITALIAN WINES:** SOAVE CLASSICO, CHARDONNAY (TUSCANY, PIEDMONT) ※ **ALTERNATIVE WINES:** SÉMILLION-CHARDONNAY (UNITED STATES, AUSTRALIA), WHITE RHÔNE BLENDS (FRANCE, AUSTRALIA, UNITED STATES)

Ripieno di spinaci, ricotta, e prosciutto

SPINACH, RICOTTA, AND PROSCIUTTO FILLING

2 pounds fresh spinach, or 2 packages (10 ounces each) frozen chopped
   spinach, thawed

¼ cup unsalted butter

1½ cups (about ¾ pound) ricotta cheese, drained in a sieve for 4 hours

2 eggs, lightly beaten

¼ pound sliced prosciutto, chopped

½ teaspoon salt

½ teaspoon freshly ground black pepper

¼ teaspoon freshly grated nutmeg, or to taste

If using fresh spinach, rinse it well, then place it in a saucepan with the rinsing water clinging to the leaves and cook until wilted, 3 to 5 minutes. Drain well, squeeze out excess moisture, and chop finely. If using thawed frozen spinach, squeeze dry.

Melt the butter in a large sauté pan over medium heat and let it color just slightly. Add the spinach and toss it in the butter for a few minutes. Transfer the spinach to a bowl and add the ricotta, eggs, and prosciutto. Mix well and season with the salt, pepper, and nutmeg. Mix well again and let cool to room temperature before filling the pasta.

If making pasta rolls, follow the directions for topping and baking included with the general directions. If making cannelloni, follow the directions for shaping and placing in a baking dish, then drizzle with melted unsalted butter, top with a little tomato sauce (page 69), and heat in the oven as directed.

MATCHING POINTER: This omniversatile filling is so easy for wine, it is almost impossible to make a mistake. Not too big (as a red) and not too oaky (red or white) and you're fine. Rosés and sparkling wines are harmonious, too. ☀ **ITALIAN WINES**: GHEMME OR SPANNA (PIEDMONT), CHIANTI CLASSICO ☀ **ALTERNATIVE WINES:** CABERNET FRANC (FRANCE, UNITED STATES), SHIRAZ AND CABERNET SAUVIGNON BLENDS (AUSTRALIA)

Ripieno di carne
MEAT FILLING

¼ cup unsalted butter

¾ pound ground veal or beef

¼ pound ground pork

½ pound ground chicken breast

Small handful (about ½ ounce) dried porcini mushrooms, soaked in hot water to soften for 30 minutes, drained with liquid reserved, and chopped

½ cup dry white wine

¼ cup chopped fresh flat-leaf parsley

Salt and freshly ground black pepper

Melt the butter in a large sauté pan over medium heat. Add the veal or beef, pork, and chicken and sauté, breaking up the meats with a fork, until they lose their redness, about 5 minutes.

Meanwhile, strain the mushroom soaking liquid through a cheesecloth-lined sieve. When the meats are ready, add the mushrooms, strained liquid, and the wine and cook until the liquids are absorbed into the meat, 5 to 8 minutes longer. Add the parsley and season with salt and pepper. Remove from the heat and let cool to room temperature before filling the pasta.

If making pasta rolls, follow the directions for topping and baking included with the general directions. If making cannelloni, follow the directions for shaping and placing in a baking dish, then cover with tomato sauce (page 69) made with ¾ cup cream, sprinkle with grated Parmesan cheese, and heat in the oven as directed.

MATCHING POINTER: A classic dish demands a classic wine. Rich, moderately robust selections based on Nebbiolo, Sangiovese, or Barbera are excellent, although something softer and rounder (Dolcetto or Bardolino) is acceptable, too. ❋ **ITALIAN WINES:** BARBERA D'ALBA, MODERATELY AGED BARBARESCO ❋ **ALTERNATIVE WINES:** RIOJA OR SIMILAR SPANISH TEMPRANILLO WINE, PINOT NOIR FOR FULLER, RICHER STYLE

Cannelloni

STUFFED PASTA TUBES

Cannelloni too often have been burdened with a poor reputation due to the
many sad examples of this well-known preparation served in second-rate Italian restaurants.
But assembled from homemade pasta sheets and a filling composed of top-notch ingredients,
these familiar stuffed pastas become a true delicacy.

<u>Makes 16; serves 8</u>

To shape, cook, and serve cannelloni: Make the Basic Egg Pasta dough (page 66), divide into 2 disks, and let rest as directed. Make one of the pasta fillings on pages 72-74. Roll out the dough, cut into squares or rectangles, and then cook as directed. Divide the filling evenly among the pasta pieces, roll up, and place seam side down in a single layer in a buttered baking dish. Top as directed in filling recipes, cover the dish, and bake in a preheated 450°F oven until heated through, 10 to 15 minutes.

<u>Note</u>: Many of these fillings will also work for ravioli. Cook the ravioli until al dente, drain well, and transfer to a buttered baking dish. Top with melted butter and Parmesan or tomato sauce, or besciamella and tomato sauce.

※

Pasta al forno alla bolognese
OVEN-BAKED PASTA WITH CLASSIC BOLOGNESE SAUCE

Giovanni Serrazanetti at Cantina Bentivoglio, in Bologna, sent me recipes for fresh pasta, fillings for tortelloni, and this classic recipe for ragù alla bolognese, which, along with salsa besciamella, the classic Italian cream sauce, can be used for making pasta al forno in the style of Bologna. You may use these sauces to assemble a fine lasagne alla bolognese as well.

※

Ragù alla bolognese tradizionale
CLASSIC BOLOGNESE SAUCE

<u>*Makes about 2 cups*</u>

3 tablespoons unsalted butter

3 tablespoons extra-virgin olive oil

½ pound ground beef

2 ounces prosciutto, chopped

2 ounces pancetta, chopped

1 celery stalk, chopped

1 carrot, peeled and chopped

1 onion, chopped

1 tablespoon tomato paste diluted in ½ cup water

¼ cup tomato purée (optional)

2 cups dry red wine

Salt and freshly ground black pepper

Melt the butter with the olive oil in a large sauté pan over medium heat. Add the beef, prosciutto, pancetta, celery, carrot, and onion and sauté, stirring often, until the vegetables are soft and lightly golden, about 15 minutes. Stir in the diluted tomato paste, the tomato pureé, if using, and the wine. Reduce the heat to low, cover, and simmer for 1½ hours.

The sauce should be very thick and richly condensed after the long simmering. Check from time to time to see if it needs more liquid, and add wine or water as needed. Season with salt and pepper.

To Make *Pasta al forno*/Oven-Baked Pasta: Preheat the oven to 400°F. Cook ¾ pound dried pasta such as penne or other tubular pasta until al dente. Drain and toss with the bolognese sauce. Divide among 4 individual buttered gratin dishes. Spread the top of each with ¼ cup of the cream sauce and sprinkle with grated Parmesan cheese. Bake until hot and golden, 12 to 15 minutes.

To Make *Lasagne al forno alla bolognese*/Lasagna Bolognese: Double the recipe for the bolognese sauce and for the cream sauce. Have 1 cup grated Parmesan cheese on hand. Make, cook, and drain lasagna noodles as directed in Basic Egg Pasta (page 66). Preheat the oven to 400°F. Butter a 9-by-12-by-3-inch baking dish. Spread a thin layer of bolognese sauce on the bottom of the dish. Add a layer of cooked noodles, overlapping them slightly; top with some bolognese sauce and a layer of cream sauce. Sprinkle with some of the Parmesan. Repeat the layers, beginning with noodles and ending with the cheese, until all of both sauces and the noodles are used. You will want at least 4 layers. Dot the top with bits of room-temperature unsalted butter. Bake until heated through and bubbling at the edges, about 25 minutes. Remove from the oven and let rest for 10 minutes, then cut into 8 to 12 portions. To reheat individual portions, place in a baking dish, cover with aluminum foil, and place in a 450°F oven until hot.

MATCHING POINTER: *Not significantly different from the profile described for the meat filling (page 74). If one can locate a wine from the region, it would be fun, but it isn't necessary.* ☀ **ITALIAN WINES:** HIGH-QUALITY RED LAMBRUSCO, NEBBIOLO D'ALBA ☀ **ALTERNATIVE WINES:** LIGHTER, MEDIUM-BODIED MERLOT, CALIFORNIA INTERPRETATIONS OF ITALIAN REDS

Pasta al cartoccio con gamberi e peperoni rossi

PASTA PACKETS WITH SHRIMP AND SWEET RED PEPPERS

Enoteca Vino Vino in Venice is the casual wine-bar wing of the well-established and well-respected Ristorante Antico Martini. Thus, it has access to a full kitchen and a well-trained staff who can cook pasta to order. I loved this recipe sent to me by proprietor Emilio Baldi and wanted to find a way to adapt it for serving under simpler circumstances. I revised it by using another technique, al cartoccio. Prepare the pasta, toss with sauce, and then if you cannot serve it at once, divide it into portions and seal each in an oiled foil or parchment packet. Then, when you need them, slip them briefly into a very hot oven.

<u>Serves 6</u>

3 large or 4 medium red bell peppers

2 green onions, each trimmed and cut into 3 or 4 pieces, or ½ small onion, coarsely chopped

7 fresh thyme sprigs

1 bay leaf

1 cup fish stock

3 tablespoons extra-virgin olive oil

1 pound medium-sized shrimp, peeled and deveined

4 cloves garlic, smashed

2 tablespoons Cognac

Salt and freshly ground black pepper

1 pound dried short pasta such as penne or fusilli

¼ cup unsalted butter, cut into bits

Combine the bell peppers, onion, 1 thyme sprig, and the bay leaf in a saucepan with water to cover. Bring to a gentle boil and cook, uncovered, until the peppers are very tender, about 1 hour. Drain, reserving only the peppers. Remove and discard the stems from the peppers and then pass them through a food mill placed over a sauté pan.

Add the fish stock to the pepper purée and stir to combine. Place over low heat and heat gently. Meanwhile, warm the olive oil in a sauté pan over medium-high heat. Add the shrimp and garlic and sauté quickly until the shrimp begin to turn pink, about 2 minutes. Pour in the Cognac and ignite with a long match. When the flames die, add the shrimp to the red pepper purée. Season with salt and pepper and remove from the heat.

Bring a large pot filled with salted water to a boil. Add the pasta and cook until al dente; the timing will depend on the pasta used. Drain and toss with the sauce.

Cut out six 10-inch squares of aluminum foil or parchment paper and oil them on one side. Top the oiled sides with the sauced pasta, dividing evenly. Dot the pasta with the butter, and then place 1 thyme sprig on each pasta portion. Bring up the sides of the foil or parchment, fold over, and seal securely. The packets can be kept for up to 4 hours in the refrigerator before reheating.

When ready to serve, preheat the oven to 450°F. Place the packets on a baking sheet and bake until heated through, 5 to 8 minutes. Let diners open their own packets.

MATCHING POINTER: *The shrimp and red bell peppers mandate a wine of substance and ripe fruit. While a juicy red wine is fine, whites and rosés may be preferable. The garlic demands an earth element in the beverage.* ❋ **ITALIAN WINES:** GRIGNOLINO, GAVI DI CORTESE ❋ **ALTERNATIVE WINES:** "VIN GRIS" OF PINOT NOIR (FRANCE, CALIFORNIA), UNOAKED CHABLIS-STYLE CHARDONNAY

Maccheroni al porro, salsicce, e porcini

PASTA GRATIN WITH LEEKS, SAUSAGES, AND MUSHROOMS

At the Enoteca Cantoniere Romana in Cividale del Friuli, this wonderful dish is made with fresh porcini. That would be a considerable luxury for most of us, but fresh cultivated mushrooms augmented with some dried porcini for flavor make a satisfying pasta gratin.

<u>Serves 8</u>

1 pound rigatoni, penne, or other macaroni

7 tablespoons olive oil

4 large leeks, or 6 smaller leeks

4 tablespoons unsalted butter

Salt and freshly ground black pepper

Freshly grated nutmeg

1 pound sweet Italian sausages, casings removed and meat crumbled

1 pound fresh mushrooms, sliced

2 cups Classic Cream Sauce (page 69)

Small handful (about ½ ounce) dried porcini mushrooms, soaked in hot water to soften for 30 minutes, drained with liquid reserved and strained through a cheesecloth-lined sieve, and mushrooms chopped (optional)

1 cup grated Parmesan cheese

Bring a large pot filled with salted water to a boil. Add the pasta and cook until al dente; the timing will depend on the type of pasta used. Drain and toss with 2 tablespoons of the olive oil. Set aside.

Meanwhile, cut off most of the green from the leeks, and then cut the leeks in half lengthwise. Cut the halves crosswise into pieces about ¾ inch wide. Place in a deep bowl of cold water, and let the dirt settle to the bottom. Using a wire skimmer or slotted spoon, transfer to a clean bowl.

Melt 2 tablespoons of the butter with 2 tablespoons of the olive oil in a large saucepan. Add the leeks and sauté, adding a bit of water as needed to moisten, until tender and cooked through, 10 to 15 minutes. Season with salt, pepper, and nutmeg, remove from the heat, and set aside.

Warm 1 tablespoon of the olive oil in a nonstick sauté pan over medium-high heat. Add the sausage and fry until cooked through and golden, about 5 minutes. Using a slotted spoon, transfer to a bowl and set aside.

For the fresh mushrooms, warm the remaining 2 tablespoons butter and 2 tablespoons olive oil in a large sauté pan over high heat. Add the fresh mushrooms and sauté, stirring occasionally, until they give off their liquid, about 6 minutes. Add the cream sauce and the porcini and their soaking liquid, if using. Season with salt, pepper, and nutmeg. Fold in the cooked leeks, the cooked sausage, ½ cup of the Parmesan, and the cooked pasta. Mix well.

Divide among 8 buttered ramekins. Top evenly with the remaining ½ cup Parmesan cheese. Bake until golden and bubbling, about 15 minutes. Serve at once.

Maccheroni con polpette/Pasta with Meatballs: Toss 1 pound cooked pasta with 1 pound batch of Little Pork Meatballs (page 123), 3 cups Tomato Sauce (page 69), ½ pound diced mozzarella, 2 large sautéed diced eggplant, and ½ pound fresh ricotta, topped with ½ cup grated Parmesan. Divide among 8 buttered ramekins. Top evenly with ½ cup Parmesan cheese. Bake until golden and bubbling, about 15 minutes. Serve at once.

MATCHING POINTER: *The sausage and leeks lend a rustic character to this dish and help to define the wine. The sausage will require some tannin to counterbalance its richness. The leeks demand a light, leafy element.* ☀ **ITALIAN WINES:** AGLIANICO DEL VULTURE, SALICE SALENTINO ☀ **ALTERNATIVE WINES:** SOFTER RHÔNE BLENDS (FRANCE, CALIFORNIA), CABERNET FRANC BLENDS (FRANCE, CALIFORNIA)

Risotto al salto

RISOTTO PANCAKE

*Leftover risotto can be turned into pancakes that are cut
into wedges and sauced. They can be stuffed with cheeses, sautéed mushrooms,
and sausage. Also called* tortini di riso, *unstuffed rice pancakes are served
with a variety of sauces at the Vineria Cozzi in Bergamo Alto.*

Serves 8

RICE:

1 cup Arborio rice

1½ cups water

1 teaspoon salt

2 eggs, lightly beaten

⅓ cup grated Parmesan cheese

Freshly ground black pepper

PANCAKE:

1½ cups diced Fontina cheese

¼ cup chopped hazelnuts

1 tablespoon chopped fresh sage or marjoram

4 to 6 tablespoons unsalted butter or olive oil

To make the rice, in a saucepan combine the rice, water, and salt. Bring to a boil over high heat, cover, reduce the heat to low, and cook until the rice is tender and all the water is absorbed, 15 to 18 minutes. Stir in the eggs and Parmesan and season to taste with pepper. You probably won't need much salt, as the cheese is fairly salty. Spoon the rice mixture onto a baking sheet and refrigerate until cool.

To make the pancake, combine the cheese, nuts, and sage or marjoram in a bowl and mix well. Warm 3 tablespoons of the butter or oil in a 10-inch, nonstick sauté pan over medium heat. Add half of the rice, packing it down. Top with the cheese mixture, spreading it evenly. Then layer the remaining rice on top, pressing it down with a

fork. Cook, shaking the pan from time to time, until the bottom of the pancake is golden brown, 5 to 7 minutes.

Slide the pancake out onto a plate. Add more butter or oil to the pan as needed to prevent sticking, and return the pan to the heat. When hot, slip the pancake, browned side up, back into the pan and cook until the second side is golden, about 5 minutes longer.

Slide onto a serving platter. Let rest for a few minutes, then cut into wedges and serve warm. The wedges may also be reheated for 10 minutes in a 350°F oven.

MATCHING POINTER: *This tasty pancake is just a delivery for a sauce. If leaning toward a tomato-based sauce, look for a sharper red wine. If going with a cream base, select a zesty, flavorful white.*
☼   **ITALIAN WINES:** BARBERA D'ASTI, ROSSO DI MONTEPULCIANO, FRANCIACORTA, SOAVE   ☼
ALTERNATIVE WINES: BARBERA (CALIFORNIA), SAUVIGNON BLANC (FRANCE, NEW ZEALAND)

☼

Bomba di riso
BAKED RICE CASSEROLE FILLED
WITH SAUSAGE AND CHEESE

Instead of frying the cooked rice as for risotto al salto *(page 82), here it is baked as a bomba or timballo. What you want is a crispy golden exterior and melting cheese inside. The fillings may vary according to what you have on hand. Cheese is most often used, but little meatballs, or chopped meat or vegetables mixed with cheese, work well, too.*

<u>Serves 6</u>

RICE:
2½ cups Arborio rice
4 eggs, lightly beaten
⅓ cup grated Parmesan cheese
Salt and freshly ground black pepper
Freshly grated nutmeg to taste

FILLING:

½ pound sweet Italian sausages, or Little Pork Meatballs from Bari (page 123)

1½ cups (about ¾ pound) ricotta cheese

¾ pound fresh mozzarella cheese, cut into ½-inch cubes

½ cup diced prosciutto (optional)

1 cup shelled peas, cooked in boiling water until tender and drained (optional)

Salt and freshly ground black pepper

Preheat the oven to 350°F. Butter a 2-quart soufflé dish.

To cook the rice, bring a saucepan filled with salted water to a boil. Add the rice and boil until tender, 15 to 18 minutes. Drain well and place in a bowl. Add the eggs and Parmesan and mix well. Season with salt, pepper, and nutmeg.

To make the filling, if using the sausages, place them in a sauté pan over medium heat and cook, turning as necessary, until nicely browned and cooked through, about 10 minutes; the timing will depend on the size. Transfer to a cutting board and cut into ½-inch-thick slices. If using the meatballs, make as directed, omitting the greens.

In a bowl, combine the ricotta and mozzarella cheeses, sausage or meatballs, and the prosciutto and peas, if using, and mix well. Season with salt and pepper. Pack half of the rice mixture into the prepared dish. Top with the cheese mixture and then the remaining rice mixture, smoothing the surface.

Bake until golden, about 30 minutes. Remove from the oven and let rest for 10 minutes, then unmold onto a platter, slice, and serve. To reheat slices, place in buttered ramekins and heat in a 350°F oven for 10 minutes.

MATCHING POINTER: This simple rib-sticking dish calls for a hearty red. Anything too soft will get lost behind layers of texture and taste. ❋ **ITALIAN WINES:** SUPER TUSCAN SANGIOVESE AND CABERNET SAUVIGNON BLENDS, BARBARESCO ❋ **ALTERNATIVE WINES:** CABERNET SAUVIGNON BLENDS, MEDIUM TO MEDIUM-FULL-BODIED ZINFANDEL

Pesce e frutti di mare
FISH AND SHELLFISH

Insalata di tonno e riso **TUNA AND RICE SALAD**

Code di scampi del Tirreno **SHRIMP WRAPPED IN PANCETTA**

Carpaccio di pesce **FISH CARPACCIO**

Insalata di fagioli e gamberi **BEAN SALAD WITH SHRIMP**

Involtini di pesce spada **SICILIAN SWORDFISH ROLLS**

Baccalà mantecato **WHIPPED SALT COD**

Sarde in saor
SARDINES IN SWEET-AND-SOUR ONION MARINADE

Vongole origanate **BAKED CLAMS WITH OREGANO**

Trota affumicata alla salsa di rafano
SMOKED TROUT WITH HORSERADISH SAUCE

Tiella di cozze **GRATIN OF MUSSELS, RICE, AND POTATOES**

left: *Vongole origanate*
BAKED CLAMS WITH OREGANO, page 104

Pesce e frutti di mare
FISH AND SHELLFISH

COOKING FISH TO ORDER requires split-second timing and finesse. A busy wine bar with a small kitchen cannot risk ruining delicate, and often costly, fish. Storage is also a concern. Fish and shellfish require ample refrigeration space and repeated icing. Although oysters are a superb match with wine, opening them to order may not be practical either. Therefore, most enoteca owners rely on a variety of smoked and cured fish and a few simple preparations that can be assembled ahead of time and brought to the table without loss of flavor and texture. The ideal menu has a balance between chilled or room-temperature dishes and those that can be reheated quickly.

Pesce affumicato, or "smoked fish," is a large menu category, with smoked salmon, tuna, swordfish, trout, sturgeon, and eel among the choices. *Bottarga*, the air-cured roe of mullet (*muggine*) or tuna (*tonno*), is another option. It is typically shaved into thin slices and strewn atop a salad of marinated onions or over platters of sliced San Marzano tomatoes, alone or with *mozzarella di bufala*, and then drizzled with extra-virgin olive oil. In an upscale establishment, a caviar selection with appropriate service will be available. Fish carpaccio, essentially *pesce crudo* (raw fish), is also an ideal dish for an enoteca. Slices of raw tuna, salmon, or swordfish are pounded until very thin and served with extra-virgin olive oil and a wedge of lemon.

Fish is also served as part of a salad, with tuna or shellfish commonly augmenting bean or rice salads. Some enoteca kitchens serve fish in marinades. Tuna, sardines, or anchovies are doused in lemon and olive oil, *salsa verde*, or capers and onions, or they are covered with a marinade of sweet-and-sour onions, *in saor*. Marinated salmon with tomatoes and onions and marinated herring with onions are popular menu items. Adventurous cooks pair seafood with fruit, such as salt cod marinated with grapefruit; eel with apple, endive, orange-infused olive oil, and balsamic vinegar; or smoked trout with horseradish sauce, garnished with chopped apple.

Other dishes require only a little advance preparation and a quick heating. *Code di scampi del Tirreno* are large shrimp wrapped in pancetta and baked for a few minutes. *Vongole origanate*, clams seasoned with oregano and baked under a crown of golden bread crumbs, and *tiella di cozze*, a gratin of mussels, rice, and potatoes from Apulia, require only a few minutes in a hot oven or under a broiler to come to the table, bubbling and fragrant. *Involtini di pesce spada*, swordfish fillets rolled around a savory filling, are usually served at room temperature or may be heated briefly in their sauce, along with a few slices of grilled eggplant or peppers.

❊

Insalata di tonno e riso

TUNA AND RICE SALAD

Grain-based salads are ideal platforms for showing off such star players as fish or shellfish. They hold up well at room temperature, too, making them perfect candidates for the enoteca menu. Usually dressed with extra-virgin olive oil and fresh lemon juice and/or a touch of mild vinegar, grain salads pair well with wine. Canned tuna has always been the most popular topping, because the Italian product is so superb. You can, of course, use fresh tuna, grilled to medium, or a medley of cooked shellfish such as shrimp, mussels, and squid. Anchovy fillets or marinated roasted peppers can be placed atop the rice just before serving, and when the season is right, ripe tomato wedges or some diced tomato can become part of the salad.

Although it may seem sacrilegious, I prefer basmati rice over Arborio for salads, as it holds its texture for a long time. Instead of rice, you can use cooked farro, *a soft wheat berry, also known as spelt, that was common in the days of the Roman Empire and has experienced a comeback in recent times. It has a lovely toothsome texture and a bigger taste presence.*

Serves 4

RICE:

1 cup long-grain white rice, preferably basmati

1½ cups water

1 teaspoon salt

VINAIGRETTE:

⅔ cup extra-virgin olive oil

2 tablespoons mild red wine vinegar

¼ cup fresh lemon juice

Salt and freshly ground black pepper

½ cup finely chopped red onion

¼ cup chopped fresh flat-leaf parsley

10 to 12 ounces olive oil–packed Italian tuna or cooked fresh tuna (see note)

8 olive oil–packed anchovy fillets, drained and cut into narrow strips or chopped (optional)

1 red bell pepper, roasted, peeled, seeded, and cut into long, narrow strips or coarsely
   diced (optional)
Tomato wedges (optional)

To make the rice, in a saucepan, combine the rice, water, and salt. Bring to a boil over high heat, cover, reduce the heat to low, and cook until the rice is tender and all the water is absorbed, 15 to 18 minutes.

Meanwhile, make the vinaigrette: In a small bowl, whisk together the olive oil, vinegar, and lemon juice. Season with salt and pepper.

Transfer the warm rice to a bowl. Drizzle with some of the vinaigrette, toss well with a fork, and let cool. Fold the onion and parsley into the cooled rice, then toss again with a fork to fluff. In another bowl, break the tuna into large chunks with your fingers and toss with some of the remaining vinaigrette.

At serving time, spoon a mound of rice onto each of 4 individual serving plates. Top with the dressed tuna; anchovies, if you like them; and the roasted pepper, if using. Drizzle with the last of the vinaigrette. (Alternatively, arrange on a single large platter, family style.) Garnish with tomato wedges, if desired.

Notes: The best Italian canned tuna is labeled _ventresca di tonno_, and it comes packed in good olive oil. Using it will make the difference between a good salad and a great salad. To cook fresh albacore tuna, brush with oil, sprinkle with salt and freshly ground black pepper, and broil or grill for about 4 minutes on each side for medium.

MATCHING POINTER: *Ample reds will clash, but the rest of the palette of wines is open and available. Shellfish generally like to be highlighted, while the rice provides the medium for a more full-bodied choice. If incorporating mussels or anchovies, steer clear of reds.* ✢ **ITALIAN WINES:** SOAVE, PINOT NERO (NORTHEAST) ✢ **ALTERNATIVE WINES:** PINOT NOIR (FRANCE, NEW WORLD), SAUVIGNON BLANC (ANYWHERE)

✳

Code di scampi del Tirreno

SHRIMP WRAPPED IN PANCETTA

This recipe was sent by Giovanni Rotti from his Enoteca Giovanni in Montecatini Terme, in Tuscany. Alas, his recipe uses a special Tuscan ingredient, lardo, *a cured meat that we cannot obtain. It is the subcutaneous fat from the shoulder or flank of the pig, sometimes preserved with herbs. Sliced paper-thin, it is typically draped atop a slice of warm bread, where it softens and almost melts. To give an idea of how special it is, I need only recall the huge Slow Food exposition I attended in 1998, in Turin. There were 345 food stands at the show, and the first to run out of samples was the one featuring* lardo di Colonnata. *But, unless the meat-import laws change, we must use pancetta for this recipe.*

Serves 4

¼ cup extra-virgin olive oil
12 jumbo shrimp, peeled and deveined
¼ cup Cognac
12 paper-thin slices pancetta (not too lean)

Preheat the oven to 475°F.

Warm the olive oil in a large sauté pan over medium-high heat. Add the shrimp and sauté quickly until they turn pink, about 3 minutes. Transfer to a plate. Add the Cognac and deglaze the pan, scraping up the brown bits on the pan bottom. Set the pan aside off the heat.

Wrap each shrimp in a slice of pancetta and arrange on a baking sheet. Place in the oven just long enough for the fat to start to melt, 2 to 3 minutes.

Meanwhile, reheat the pan juices. When the shrimp are ready, transfer them to 4 individual serving plates, top with the pan juices, and serve at once.

MATCHING POINTER: *The pancetta steers the dish toward rosé or light-bodied reds. How mild the shrimp are should guide your choice.* ✳ **ITALIAN WINES:** FREISA (PIEDMONT), CERASUOLO (ABRUZZO) ✳ **ALTERNATIVE WINES:** ROSÉ (PROVENCE), NAPA GAMAY (CALIFORNIA)

Carpaccio di pesce

FISH CARPACCIO

Long before fish tartare and fish carpaccio hit the menu of every fashionable restaurant, there was simply pesce crudo, *or sliced raw fish. At the popular Enoteca L'Arco del Re in Ancona, the kitchen assembles swordfish carpaccio, while the Osteria Vivaldi in Venice offers salmon carpaccio. A rich fish such as Alaskan halibut would be good, too. But all of these fish require a bit of time in a marinade to "cure" them partially. Given the fish selection at the markets I frequent, tuna is almost always my first choice, as it requires no marinating. Settle for nothing less than the freshest fish.*

Serves 4

4 slices ahi tuna, 3 ounces each

½ cup extra-virgin olive oil

¼ cup fresh lemon juice

1 tablespoon brandy (optional)

1 tablespoon Dijon mustard (optional)

Salt and freshly ground black pepper

2 bunches watercress or young, tender arugula, tough stems removed

Paper-thin slices of black or red radishes or daikon

2 tablespoons chopped fresh chives

Place each slice of tuna between 2 sheets of lightly oiled parchment paper or plastic wrap, and pound very gently to uniform thinness. The fish is already tender, so don't be too exuberant. Refrigerate, still in the paper, until needed.

To make a vinaigrette, in a bowl, whisk together the olive oil, lemon juice, brandy or mustard (if using), and salt and pepper to taste.

To serve, in a bowl, toss the watercress or arugula with ¼ cup of the vinaigrette. Arrange the greens in a circular pattern on 4 salad plates. Drain the radish slices and arrange atop the greens, placing them at the outer edges of the plate. Peel away the top sheet of paper from one side of the tuna and invert the tuna carefully atop the greens. Peel away the second sheet of oiled paper. Push the tuna down onto the plate. It is crucial that you sprinkle the tuna lightly with salt, or it will taste flat. Drizzle the remaining vinaigrette on top. Sprinkle with the chopped chives and serve.

MATCHING POINTER: *Clean, zesty white wines with forward citrus fruit and lemony acidity are best for underscoring the simplicity and inherent sweetness of the fish. The more current the vintage, the better.* ❖ **ITALIAN WINES:** ARNEIS, SAUVIGNON BLANC/VERDUZZO (FRIULI) ❖ **ALTERNATIVE WINES:** VINHO VERDE (PORTUGAL), MUSCADET (FRANCE), SAUVIGNON BLANC (CALIFORNIA)

❋

Insalata di fagioli e gamberi
BEAN SALAD WITH SHRIMP

Although the Tuscans are known as the mangiafagioli, *or bean eaters, everyone in Italy eats beans. They are a basic component of many soups, stews, and salads, and because they are so neutral in flavor, they provide a fine background for more dramatic flavors. This room-temperature bean-based dish is a classic at enotecas. It may be topped with high-quality canned tuna and chopped or shaved red onions, but it is often made a bit more upscale by using cooked shellfish such as shrimp or lobster.*

The Ostaria Antico Dolo in Venice uses baby octopus and adds chopped celery to the white bean salad.

Serves 6

1½ cups dried Great Northern or cannellini beans

2 quarts water

3 teaspoons salt, plus salt to taste

⅓ cup plus ½ cup virgin olive oil, plus more for sautéing and drizzling

3 to 4 tablespoons fresh lemon juice or a mild wine vinegar, or to taste

½ teaspoon freshly ground black pepper, plus pepper to taste

1 cup finely chopped red onion

1 cup chopped vine-ripened tomatoes

4 tablespoons chopped fresh herbs such as basil, mint, or flat-leaf parsley

24 large or medium-sized shrimp, peeled and deveined

To prepare the beans, pick them over, rinse well, place them in a bowl with water to cover generously, and soak overnight. The next day, drain the beans and place in a saucepan with the 2 quarts water. Bring to a boil over medium-high heat, reduce the heat to low, cover, and simmer until tender but not soft, about 40 minutes. Add 2 teaspoons of the salt during the last 15 minutes of cooking. Remove from the heat; you should have about 3 cups cooked beans. (The beans can be used for soups and stews as well as salads.)

Drain the beans and transfer to a bowl. While they are still warm, toss with the 1/3 cup olive oil, 3 to 4 tablespoons lemon juice or vinegar, 1 teaspoon salt, and the 1/2 teaspoon pepper. Let the beans cool and absorb the flavor of the dressing. When cool, add the remaining 1/2 cup olive oil, the onion, the tomatoes, and 2 tablespoons of the herbs. Mix well, then taste and adjust the seasoning with salt and pepper. You may want to add a bit more lemon juice or vinegar too.

Pour enough olive oil into a sauté pan to form a light film on the bottom and place over high heat. When it is hot, add the shrimp and sauté quickly until pink and cooked through, 3 to 4 minutes.

To serve, spoon the beans into an attractive serving dish. Arrange the shrimp on top, sprinkle with a little salt, and drizzle with a bit of olive oil or with lemon juice or vinegar and oil. Top with the remaining 2 tablespoons chopped herbs.

MATCHING POINTER: *The creaminess and waxy texture of the dish calls for similar elements in a white wine. The inherent sweetness of shrimp and the high acid of tomatoes must be matched, too. If your onions are very "oniony," you may want to increase the earthiness of the wine.* ✣ **ITALIAN WINES:** GRECO DI TUFO, CHARDONNAY (FRIULI, TUSCANY) ✣ **ALTERNATIVE WINES:** CHARDONNAY (FRENCH BURGUNDY), OFF-DRY OR DRY RIESLING (ALSACE, CALIFORNIA)

Involtini di pesce spada

SICILIAN SWORDFISH ROLLS

Involtini di pesce spada *are a specialty of the Hostaria del Vicolo in Sciaccia,*
in southern Sicily. The use of pine nuts and currants in the recipe can be ascribed to the
arrival of the Arabs on the island in the ninth century. The swordfish rolls can be baked
or grilled, and may be served warm or at room temperature. The accompanying sauce, called
salmoriglio, *is a popular dressing for fish from Naples south through Sicily. The same filling*
is used to stuff sardines in another Sicilian classic, sarde a beccafico, *a favorite of the*
residents of Palermo. A beccafico *is a tiny bird that eats figs while the fruits are still on the*
tree. The sardine dish was given this name because the fish rolls recall the little, overstuffed
birds. Like the swordfish rolls, they are baked with bay leaves.

12 slices swordfish, each about ¼ inch thick (about 2 pounds total)
Salt

FILLING:
About 1½ cups diced coarse country bread (crusts removed)
9 tablespoons olive oil
Salt and freshly ground black pepper
1 onion, chopped
2 anchovy fillets, chopped (optional)
¼ cup dried currants, plumped in hot water and drained
¼ cup pine nuts, toasted
¼ cup chopped fresh flat-leaf parsley
¼ cup fresh lemon juice
¼ cup fresh orange juice
4 to 6 bay leaves
2 teaspoons dried oregano

SALMORIGLIO SAUCE:
2 tablespoons dried oregano
2 teaspoons finely minced garlic
¼ cup virgin olive oil
3 tablespoons fresh lemon juice
½ teaspoon salt
½ teaspoon freshly ground black pepper
2 tablespoons chopped fresh flat-leaf parsley
½ cup mild olive oil

Place each slice of swordfish between 2 sheets of lightly oiled parchment paper or plastic wrap, and pound very gently to uniform thinness. Each slice should be about 5 inches long and 3 inches wide. Trim as necessary. Any odd fragments of swordfish can be incorporated into the filling. Peel off the top sheet of parchment or plastic and sprinkle the fish with salt. Refrigerate until needed.

To make the filling, first make bread crumbs: Preheat the oven to 350°F. Pulse the bread cubes in a food processor until you have fine crumbs. Spread the crumbs on a baking sheet. Drizzle evenly with 3 tablespoons of the olive oil and season with salt and pepper. Toss well to coat. Bake, stirring occasionally, until golden, about 20 minutes. Remove from the oven and measure out ⅔ cup of the crumbs. Reserve any leftover crumbs for another use. Raise the oven temperature to 400°F.

To make the filling, heat 4 tablespoons of the olive oil in a small sauté pan and cook the onion (and any fish remnants) until soft, about 10 minutes. Stir in the ⅔ cup bread crumbs, anchovy (if using), currants, pine nuts, parsley, and half each of the lemon juice and orange juice. Season with salt and pepper, remove from the heat, and let cool.

Oil a 9-by-12-inch baking dish. Place a heaping tablespoon of filling on each swordfish slice and roll up. Secure with a toothpick or kitchen string. Arrange the swordfish rolls side by side in the baking dish, interspersing the bay leaves between the rolls. Sprinkle with the oregano. Drizzle with the remaining 2 tablespoons olive oil and the remaining lemon and orange juices.

Bake until the fish is cooked through, 12 to 15 minutes. While the swordfish rolls are baking, make the sauce: Combine the oregano and garlic in a mortar. Grind with a pestle and gradually add the virgin olive oil to make a paste. Add the lemon juice, salt, pepper, and parsley and mix well. Gradually beat in the mild olive oil. (You can also make this sauce in a blender.) Transfer the swordfish rolls to a platter and serve warm or at room temperature drizzled with the sauce.

MATCHING POINTER: *The currants, orange juice, and toasted pine nuts add a sweetness that makes an off-dry selection a welcome match. The meaty character of the swordfish must be matched, too.*
✢ **ITALIAN WINES:** VERMENTINO (SARDINIA), VERNACCIA (SAN GIMIGNANO, ORISTANO, SERRAPETRONA), SAUVIGNON BLANC (FRIULI) ✢ **ALTERNATIVE WINES:** CHENIN BLANC (SOUTH AFRICA, FRANCE), SAUVIGNON AND SÉMILLON BLENDS (FRANCE, AUSTRALIA, WASHINGTON STATE)

✳

Baccalà mantecato

WHIPPED SALT COD

Baccalà mantecato is a signature dish of Venice. It is served in almost all the local bacari *(wine bars), so I was not surprised when every enoteca in the Veneto that responded to my inquiry sent a recipe for this purée of salt cod whipped with olive oil.*

Baccalà mantecato may be served on grilled bread or on grilled, baked, or fried polenta crostini, but it is sensational spooned atop soft, warm polenta. And if you are feeling extravagant, crown this duo of warm and cool with a dollop of osetra caviar.

<u>Serves 6 to 8</u>

SALT COD:

2 pounds boneless salt cod

Milk for cooking (optional), plus about ½ cup milk, heated, if needed

½ cup extra-virgin olive oil, or as needed

3 cloves garlic, finely minced

2 tablespoons chopped fresh flat-leaf parsley

Salt and freshly ground black pepper

POLENTA:

1 cup white or yellow polenta

4 cups water

Salt and freshly ground black pepper

¼ cup unsalted butter, at room temperaturer

6 tablespoons osetra caviar (optional)

To prepare the salt cod, combine the fish with water to cover in a bowl. Refrigerate for 1 to 2 days, changing the water at least 3 times. The length of soaking necessary will depend on the saltiness of the cod; thicker pieces will take longer.

Drain the salt cod and place in a saucepan. Add water or equal parts water and milk to cover and bring slowly to a gentle simmer. Cook until the fish is tender, about

10 minutes. Drain the salt cod and let cool slightly, then flake the fish with your fingers, removing any errant bones, traces of skin, or discolored or tough parts.

Place the fish in a food processor or the bowl of an electric mixer fitted with the paddle attachment and process or mix to break up the pieces into finer shreds. Gradually beat in as much olive oil as needed for a smooth purée. Taste the fish. It is unlikely that it will be too salty, but if it is, whip in some warm milk. Transfer the fish to a bowl and fold in the garlic and parsley. Season with pepper. Don't be surprised if you need to add a bit of salt for balance.

While the salt cod is simmering, begin making the polenta: Combine the polenta and water in a heavy-bottomed saucepan and place over medium heat. Bring slowly to a boil, stirring often to prevent lumps from forming. Reduce the heat to low and simmer, stirring often, until the polenta is thick and no longer grainy on the tongue, about 30 minutes. Whisk in salt and pepper to taste and the butter. To keep the polenta warm until serving, transfer it to the top pan of a double boiler placed over hot water. If it thickens too much before serving, whisk in hot water until a creamy consistency forms once again.

To serve, spoon the warm polenta on individual serving plates. Place a dollop of salt cod on top of each, positioning it slightly off to one side. Top with the caviar if you like—and how could you not!

Polenta Crostini: If you like, serve the salt cod on polenta _crostini_. Cook the polenta as directed, then spread it in an oiled 9-by-12-inch baking dish. It should be about ¼ inch thick. Refrigerate until firm, then cut into desired shapes (squares, rounds, or rectangles). Brush lightly with olive oil on both sides and place over a charcoal fire or under a preheated broiler and grill or broil, turning once, until golden and crisp. Alternatively, fry in olive oil in a frying pan, or arrange on an oiled baking sheet and heat in a 400°F oven until hot.

MATCHING POINTER: _When pairing wine with salt cod, high acidity is a must, and a hint of earthiness is warranted to accent the inherent rusticity of the fish (plus the garlic). The addition of polenta, with its toasted grain flavor, allows for light oak treatments._ ❖ **ITALIAN WINES:** CHARDONNAY (TUSCANY, PIEDMONT), VERDICCHIO ❖ **ALTERNATIVE WINES:** MODERATELY OAKED CHARDONNAY (ANYWHERE), RUEDA (SPAIN)

※

Sarde in saor

SARDINES IN SWEET-AND-SOUR ONION MARINADE

Saor is Venetian dialect for sapore, *or "flavor." Another term for this style of dish is* in carpione, *in a mild vinegar marinade, or* con cipollata, *"with onion." For this Venetian classic, sautéed fish is marinated under a layer of sweet-and-sour onions. It is served in the traditional manner, at room temperature, in the city at Enoteca Vino Vino and at Roberto Meneghetti's combination* osteria *and wine bar, Osteria al Bacco. Matteo Ruffini, at the Osteria Antico Dolo, also in Venice, departs from custom by serving the marinated sardines on a bed of warm, soft polenta. If you cannot find fresh sardines, use small, firm fish fillets instead.*

<u>Serves 4 to 6</u>

¼ cup olive oil, plus more for frying

4 large onions, sliced ¼ inch thick

¼ cup white wine vinegar

¼ cup raisins, plumped in hot water and drained (optional)

¼ cup pine nuts, toasted

1 teaspoon salt, plus salt to taste

½ teaspoon freshly ground black pepper, plus pepper to taste

2 pounds fresh sardines, or 1½ pounds firm fish fillets such as sole

Warm the ¼ cup olive oil in a large sauté pan over medium heat. Add the onions and cook, stirring occasionally, until tender and lightly golden, about 20 minutes. Add the vinegar, the raisins, if using, and the pine nuts and cook for a few minutes longer to blend the flavors. Season with the 1 teaspoon salt and ½ teaspoon pepper and set aside.

If using the sardines, clean them, remove their heads, and remove their backbones as well, but leave the fillets attached. Rinse well and open each fish flat, as if it were a book. Dry thoroughly with paper towels. Season with salt and pepper. If using fish fillets, rinse, pat dry, and season with salt and pepper.

Pour enough olive oil into a large sauté pan to film the bottom and place over medium–high heat. When hot, add the fish in batches and fry, turning once, until golden on both sides and cooked through, 5 to 6 minutes.

Using a slotted spatula, carefully transfer the cooked fish to a platter and top with the onion mixture. Cover and marinate in the refrigerator for 24 hours. To serve, bring to room temperature.

MATCHING POINTER: *This dish is at its finest with light, fruit-forward red wines, not unlike many of those in the Veneto. Don't overlook the sweet-sour character of the dish, which lends itself to off-dry whites (or rosés). Finally, if you serve the sardines with polenta, select a richer (more generous) wine.* ✧ **ITALIAN WINES:** VALPOLICELLA, MERLOT (VENETO) ✧ **ALTERNATIVE WINES:** PINOT NOIR (CALIFORNIA, OREGON), VOUVRAY

❉

Vongole origanate

BAKED CLAMS WITH OREGANO

A perfect small plate for a glass of white or sparkling wine. What makes the dish special is texture: the crunchiness of the toasted bread crumbs atop the slightly chewy clams.

<u>Serves 4</u>

2 cups diced coarse country bread (crusts removed)

6 tablespoons unsalted butter, melted, or olive oil

1 teaspoon salt

½ teaspoon freshly ground black pepper, plus pepper to taste

24 medium-sized or large soft-shell clams, well scrubbed

½ cup dry white wine or water

4 cloves garlic, finely minced

¼ cup chopped fresh flat-leaf parsley

2 teaspoons dried oregano

Extra-virgin olive oil for drizzling

Lemon wedges

First, make the toasted bread crumbs: Preheat the oven to 350°F. Pulse the bread cubes in a food processor until you have fine crumbs. Spread the bread crumbs on a baking sheet. Drizzle evenly with the butter or oil, and sprinkle with the salt and ½ teaspoon pepper. Toss well to coat. Bake, stirring occasionally, until golden, about 20 minutes. Remove from the oven and measure out 1 cup of the crumbs. Reserve any leftover crumbs for another use. Raise the oven temperature to 450°F, or preheat the broiler.

Combine the clams and wine or water in a large sauté pan. Cover, place over high heat, and steam, shaking the pan a few times, until the clams open, just a few minutes. They should barely crack open. Do not overcook. Using a slotted utensil, transfer the clams, draining them well over the pan, to a large platter or tray. Discard any that failed to open.

Pour the liquid in the pan through a cheesecloth-lined sieve placed over a bowl. Discard the top shell from each clam and, using a small knife, detach the clam from the bottom shell, leaving it resting in the shell. Divide the clams among 4 gratin dishes, overlapping them a bit to keep them from tipping over. (Use flameproof dishes if broiling.) Drizzle evenly with the strained clam liquid.

In a small bowl, stir together the 1 cup bread crumbs, garlic, parsley, and oregano. Sprinkle an equal amount of the crumb mixture over each clam. Top each clam with a few grindings of pepper, and drizzle with extra-virgin olive oil.

Bake or broil until the crumbs are golden, 3 or 4 minutes. Serve immediately with the lemon wedges.

MATCHING POINTER: *Clams are surprisingly difficult to pair with wine. Their implicit brininess shatters many wines that would seem intuitively correct. Sparkling wine is excellent, as are whites with bracing levels of crisp acidity. The oregano adds a subtle wine-friendly accent.* ✣ **ITALIAN WINES:** GRECO DI TUFO, PROSECCO ✣ **ALTERNATIVE WINES:** VINHO VERDE (PORTUGAL), YOUNG SPARKLING WINE

Trota affumicata alla salsa di rafano

SMOKED TROUT WITH HORSERADISH SAUCE

Smoked fish comprises a large segment of the enoteca menu. Salsa di rafano, also known as salsa di cren *(cren is derived from Austrian dialect), is a classic horseradish sauce popular in the Veneto, Friuli, and Alto Adige. It is excellent with smoked trout and smoked salmon, as well as with cooked beets and potato pancakes, and is often served with* carne salata *(page 129), boiled beef, or as one of the accompanying sauces for* bollito misto. *Some horseradish sauces are enriched with cream and others are simply grated horseradish emulsified with vinegar and olive oil.*

Serves 4

HORSERADISH SAUCE:

About ⅓ cup peeled, thinly sliced horseradish root (sliced against the grain)

¼ cup distilled white vinegar, or as needed

½ cup sour cream

¼ cup heavy cream

2 to 3 tablespoons olive oil

⅓ cup finely minced white onion (optional)

Salt and freshly ground black pepper

¼ cup chopped walnuts, toasted (optional)

1 tart apple, peeled, halved, cored, and minced (optional)

2 bunches watercress, tough stems removed

2 smoked trout, heads, skin, and bones removed, then divided into fillets

8 little new potatoes, boiled (optional)

1 cup sliced fennel or cucumber (optional)

4 beets, boiled, peeled, halved, and then sliced (optional)

To make the sauce, place the horseradish and vinegar in a mini processor and process until a fine, smooth purée forms (see note). You should have 3 to 4 tablespoons. In a bowl, whisk together the sour cream, cream, olive oil, onion (if using), and horseradish purée. Season with salt and pepper and adjust with vinegar to taste. Add the walnuts or apple, if desired.

To serve, make a bed of watercress on 4 individual serving plates. Arrange the trout and your choice of potatoes, fennel, or beets, or all three, on top of the watercress. Drizzle the horseradish sauce over all.

<u>Note:</u> If you have only a large food processor, you will probably have difficulty processing this small amount of horseradish, so you may have to purée a larger amount to get good results. (It keeps for many weeks under refrigeration.) You may also use prepared horseradish.

MATCHING POINTER: *The sweetness of smoking points toward Riesling or other similar northeastern white grapes. Rosé provides a nice foil to the horseradish, while affording substantial refreshment.*
❖ **ITALIAN WINES:** GRIGNOLINO, ORVIETO ❖ **ALTERNATIVE WINES:** DRY TO OFF-DRY RIESLING (GERMANY, PACIFIC NORTHWEST), ALBARIÑO (SPAIN)

✳

Tiella di cozze

GRATIN OF MUSSELS, RICE, AND POTATOES

Alessandra De Candia of the Enoteca De Candia in Bari sent this classic
Apulian recipe for tiella. Potatoes, rice, and sautéed onions are combined with steamed
mussels and baked in a round ceramic dish called a tiella. The inclusion of rice is a signature of
Bari; other versions of this recipe use only potatoes. Traditionally the mussels are served on the
half shell, but for ease of eating and serving, I have taken them out of their shells.
In a second move against tradition, I have parboiled the rice to shorten the overall
cooking time, and thus guarantee that the mussels will not dry out.

<u>Serves 4</u>

⅔ cup long-grain white rice

2 pounds boiling potatoes, preferably Yukon Gold or Yellow Finn, peeled

½ cup extra-virgin olive oil

2 cups chopped onion

1 or 2 celery stalks, chopped (optional)

2 pounds mussels, scrubbed and debearded

1½ cups dry white wine

Salt and freshly ground black pepper

1 cup toasted bread crumbs (see Baked Clams with Oregano, page 104)

4 teaspoons finely minced garlic, or more to taste

½ cup chopped fresh flat-leaf parsley

⅔ cup grated pecorino cheese

Combine the rice with water to cover in a bowl and let soak for about 1 hour. Drain, transfer to a small saucepan, and add water to cover generously. Bring to a gentle boil over medium heat and cook until al dente, about 10 minutes. Drain and set aside.

Combine the potatoes with lightly salted water to cover in a saucepan. Bring to a boil and cook until almost cooked but still firm when tested with a skewer, 15 to

25 minutes. The timing will depend on their size. Be careful not to let them become too soft, as they must be firm enough to slice. Drain and set aside.

Heat ¼ cup of the olive oil in a sauté pan over medium heat. Add the onion and the celery, if using, and sauté until tender, about 10 minutes. Remove from the heat and set aside.

Arrange the mussels in a wide, shallow saucepan and pour the wine over them. Cover, place over high heat, and steam, shaking the pan a few times, until the mussels open, just a few minutes. They should barely crack open. Do not overcook. Using a slotted utensil, transfer the mussels, draining them well over the pan, to a colander. Discard any that failed to open. When the mussels are cool enough to touch, remove them from their shells, carefully pull off any beards that remain, and place the mussels in a small bowl. Pour the liquid remaining in the pan through a cheesecloth-lined sieve placed over a bowl. (If preparing in advance, strain the liquid into the bowl holding the mussels, cover, and refrigerate until ready to bake.)

To serve, preheat the oven to 375°F. Oil 8 ramekins, each with about 1-cup capacity. Slice the potatoes about ⅓ inch thick and place in a bowl. Toss with the remaining ¼ cup olive oil and sprinkle lightly with salt and pepper. Divide the potatoes evenly among the prepared ramekins, layering them neatly on the bottom. Top with the onions and then the mussels. Sprinkle evenly with the rice and drizzle about ¼ cup of the mussel liquid over each portion. In a small bowl, stir together the bread crumbs, garlic, parsley, and cheese. Sprinkle evenly over the tops of the filled ramekins.

Bake until bubbling and browned on top, 7 to 10 minutes. Let cool for a few minutes before serving.

MATCHING POINTER: *The surrounding elements take the emphasis off the mussels to carry the pairing. If your mussels are sweet rather than pungent, you can opt for a rosé. Otherwise, the potatoes and rice add a textural component that suggests more generous white wines. Steer clear of too much oak, as it will clash.* ✤ **ITALIAN WINES:** ROSÉ (FRIULI), ROSATO (COLLIO), VERDICCHIO ✤ **ALTERNATIVE WINES:** GRUNER VELTLINER (AUSTRIA), PINOT GRIS (ALSACE, OREGON)

Carne e Pollame
MEAT AND POULTRY

Stufato d'agnello alla campidanesi
LAMB STEW WITH LEMON AND GARLIC FROM CAMPIDANO

Aristà di maiale alla fiorentina   **FLORENTINE ROAST PORK LOIN**

La padellaccia   **PORK AND BORLOTTI BEAN STEW**

Polpette al barese   **LITTLE PORK MEATBALLS FROM BARI**

Carpaccio alla bagna cauda
RAW BEEF WITH OLIVE OIL, GARLIC, AND ANCHOVY

Carne salata   **SPICE-AND-SALT-CURED BEEF**

Polpettone alla romana   **ROMAN MEAT LOAF**

Tagliata di manzo al Brunello di Montalcino
SLICED STEAK WITH WINE SAUCE

Petto d'anatra all'aceto balsamico ed arancia
DUCK BREAST WITH BALSAMIC VINEGAR AND ORANGE

Galletto ripieno   **STUFFED CHICKEN BREAST**

Rollata di vitello   **STUFFED VEAL ROLL**

left: *Stufato d'agnello alla campidanesi*
LAMB STEW WITH LEMON AND GARLIC FROM CAMPIDANO, page 116

Carne e Pollame
MEAT AND POULTRY

ENOTECA OWNERS are constantly on the move, serving food, pouring wine, and talking about the wine to the guests. With little time for cooking food to order, meat and poultry preparations, like many other dishes, tend to be simple. Most are served at room temperature and a few are quickly reheated. A whole segment of the meat menu may be devoted to *carpaccio*, thin slices of raw beef or veal. They might be adorned with thinly sliced baby artichokes, sliced mushrooms, or wild arugula, then drizzled with extra-virgin olive oil and topped with shavings of Parmesan.

Most of the other sliced meats fall into the category that Americans commonly call cold cuts. How flat and dispassionate a name for some of the most truly special foods in Italy's culinary repertoire! *Salumi*, the umbrella term for the numerous cured meats and sausages produced all over Italy by large companies and small artisans, make up one of the largest sections of the enoteca menu. In a restaurant or trattoria, these meats are served as an antipasto, that is, before the meal. In an enoteca they often are the meal. Each establishment offers an assortment of locally cured products along with some specialty imports from other regions. Today, *prosciutto crudo* and *cotto*, mortadella, and *bresaola* are the only *salumi* directly imported to the United States from Italy. But many American and Canadian *salumi*, such as *sopressata*, *salame toscano*, *luganega*, *coppa*, and *capocollo*, are there for the asking.

The *salumi* selection includes pâtés, local hams, sausages, and cured meats. *Carne salata* (spiced beef) may be served with horseradish sauce, and *lingua salmistrata* (cured tongue) or boiled beef is often paired with *salsa verde*, a sauce of parsley, olive oil, garlic, and capers. These cold plates are called *affettati*, or sliced meats. *Grissini* or a rustic bread is always set alongside as an accompaniment, sometimes with a slice of impeccable sweet butter, the creaminess playing beautifully off the dry meat. The most memorable Italian *panino* is made with slices of fine prosciutto and the best sweet butter—simple, delicious, and perfect.

Cured meats are often matched with fruit, a contrast of salt and sweet. If a pairing of prosciutto and melon or prosciutto and figs is good, then salami with its extra spice and fat can be wonderful with thin slivers of pear or fig. Try the Green Tomato Conserve (page 174) in the condiment chapter with cold roast pork, slices of ham, or a plain chicken breast. The Enoteca di Cormons in Friuli serves pancetta-wrapped prunes, broiled or baked until the pancetta is barely cooked.

The most practical hot meat preparations for the enoteca kitchen are stews and roasts. A pork and bean stew from Umbria, a ragout of pork meatballs braised with greens, and a lamb stew from Sardinia are typical. Osso buco would also be a good choice. They are all fast and easy to reheat on a simple stove top or in the microwave. Larger cuts of meat, such as grilled steak, roast pork loin, or braised leg of veal, are sliced and arranged on platters with appropriate sauces such as mustard, *mostarda di frutta*, *salsa verde*, or *salsa di rafano* (page 106). Or they might be accompanied with cooked vegetables, house-preserved *sott'olio* (vegetables cooked and preserved in oil and herbs), or small green salads. Sautéed chicken or duck breasts are typically sliced and served with small salads.

Although we usually think of red wine with meat, prosciutto, cooked hams, and some cured meats are served with sparkling wines and dry whites such as Trebbiano and Verdicchio. Some salamis are served with Lambrusco, as its *frizzante* and fruity quality is a fine balance for their rich salt-cured character.

A BRIEF GUIDE TO *AFFETTATI, SALUMI,* AND *INSACCATI*

CARNE SALATA, one of the most popular of the *affettati*, is salted cured meat from the Alto Adige. You may make your own version by using the recipe on page 129.

BRESAOLA, another northern specialty, this time of the Valtellina district of Lombardy, is beef that has been cured by salting and air-drying. The high altitude and cold air of the area are perfect for preserving the meat. Fillet or loin is the cut of choice, as the meat must be lean to prevent spoilage. *Bresaola* is commonly served in paper-thin slices, dressed with lemon juice, extra-virgin olive oil, and black pepper, although it is also sometimes paired with sections of grapefruit, wild greens, and olive oil. It should not be cut too far ahead of time, or it will darken and discolor. At the Enoteca Costantini in Rome, I was treated to a plate that compared three kinds of *bresaola*: beef, horse, and deer. The horse meat was quite sweet, the deer meat rather gamey, and the beef the perfect middle taste. Some enotecas are known for their *salume di selvaggina*, the cured meats of deer, wild boar, or mountain goat.

Most **SALUMI** are made with pork. The best known of them, of course, is prosciutto, with the most renowned example *prosciutto di Parma*. Prosciutto is made from the hind thigh of the pig, and a government stamp on the rounded side of each ham attests to its being produced according to strict government regulations. Other stellar cured hams that are exported include the darker and sweeter *prosciutto di San Daniele*, from a town in Friuli, and *prosciutto di Carpegna*, from a town that borders Tuscany and the Marches. In Italy, prosciutti made by local artisans are available as well, and many of these are featured on enoteca menus.

CULATELLO, a much-prized specialty of Emilia-Romagna, is a selected segment of pork rump cured in a pig's bladder and aged for a year. A whole prosciutto is sacrificed to make it, so it is a costly treat and is not exported. The most famous is *culatello di Zibello*.

SPECK is from Alto Adige and may be made from either the belly or the leg of the pig. If it is from the belly, it is like smoked pancetta, while if the leg is used, it is like a smoked prosciutto. Although not yet imported to the United States, locally produced versions are available at our delicatessens.

LARDO is another treat that must be sampled in Italy. Creamy pork fat cured with herbs, it is usually sliced paper-thin and served on warm bread. Some of the most well-regarded products are from Colonnata in Tuscany, and Langhirano in Emilia Romagna, and from the northeastern region, Lardo d'Arnad of Val d'Aosta, where it is cured with rosemary.

PANCETTA ARROTOLATA is pork belly that is rolled, salt-cured, and seasoned with pepper and cloves, and then enclosed in a thin casing. It is a popular filling for *panini* and appears on platters of *salumi*. It is also used in cooking.

GUANCIALE, a pig's cheek cured with salt and pepper, is used a great deal in Roman cooking, in such dishes as *spaghetti alla gricia* or *alla carbonara*.

The Italian **SALAME** is a generic term for **INSACCATI,** sausages and meats in casings that Americans call salami. Some of the best known are the relatively lean *salame di Milano*, which is usually aged for three to four months, and the *salame di Fabriano*, once made only with pork and small cubes of lard, but today a mixture of pork and beef flavored with whole peppercorns and garlic. There are *salame di Napoli*, made with pork and beef; *salame toscano*, with its large eyes of fat and ample garlic and pepper; and *salame di Varzi*, sweet and delicate. *Salame felino* is considered by many *salame* enthusiasts to be the best of all. It comes from the same area that produces *prosciutto di Parma* and is made from pigs that feed on the by-products from the manufacture of Parmesan cheese. The meat is lean, medium grind, and seasoned with pepper, white wine, and garlic. It is packed into a natural casing and aged for two months.

SOPRESSA VENETA is a large—but tasty—industrial salami, while *sopressata di Calabria* is smaller, soft and spicy, and made from ground meats, fat, liver, and lungs. *Lucanica*, from Basilicata, calls for lean pork seasoned with black pepper, sweet pepper, and chili pepper. It may be eaten cooked or uncooked and is sometimes lightly smoked and kept at room temperature for a time. *Luganega*, which is derived from the same word, is a long, coiled spicy sausage made in Lombardy and the Veneto. In Apulia, *salame leccese*, from the lovely baroque town of Lecce, is composed of veal and pork and is seasoned with lemon and cinnamon. Umbria is known for *mezzafegati*, a sweet liver sausage flavored with orange, raisins, and pine nuts. The excellent *finocchiona toscana*, a soft pork salami with fennel seeds, is not to be confused with *finocchiata*, a cured pork loin sausage with pepper and wild fennel.

CAPOCOLLO is a specialty of central and southern Italy, with distinctive versions produced from Umbria to Calabria to Apulia. This salted, cured pork sausage is sometimes lightly smoked over a green oak fire and other times simply hung in a cool, well-ventilated spot to cure. At its best, it is lean and fragrant with spices.

COPPA, one of Italy's most common sausages, is rolled pig's shoulder cured in saltpeter, salt, pepper, and nutmeg. The ideal *coppa* is made with equal parts lean and fat meat and aged for three months. Mortadella, a large fully cooked, mildly seasoned sausage with big eyes of fat and sometimes pistachio nuts, is made mainly in Modena and Bologna and is now being exported to the United States.

Most **AFFETTATI** and **INSACCATI** are served cold. A few special sausages are traditionally served warm, however. At the Enoteca di Cormons, *salame nel aceto* (salami with vinegar), a classic Friulian dish, is prepared. A thick slice of young *salame friulano* is sautéed until lightly colored on both sides. The pan is deglazed with wine vinegar, and the vinegar is reduced to syrupy juices. The sautéed salami is then draped over a slice of polenta, and the juices are spooned on top. A glass of regional Merlot or Cabernet is the customary accompaniment. In Emilia-Romagna, a thick slice of young *coppa* is rubbed with herbs and slipped into the oven, where it is basted frequently with Marsala. It is then sliced and served.

COTECHINO, a fresh sausage made with the lean meat from the head and neck of the pig, is simmered for about three hours and then served with lentils, boiled beans, or mashed potatoes. It is a specialty of Modena in Emilia-Romagna. *Zampone*, another specialty of Modena, is finely chopped cuts of pork stuffed into a pig's trotter. It is also long-cooked and served hot.

POULTRY makes up only a small segment of the varied world of Italian cured meats, principally in the form of smoked duck and goose breasts from artisanal producers. Cured goose breast, *petto d'oca*, is served many ways, including thinly sliced, placed on a bed of baby arugula, and dressed with orange- or lemon-infused oil and black pepper, or tossed with sliced pears, spinach, and an herbed dressing. Duck breast may be served in a similar fashion. Top-notch establishments offer foie gras along with an assortment of terrines and pâtés. One can find duck terrine, goose terrine, duck and foie gras terrine, and pâtés of goose with cinnamon, pheasant with hazelnuts, and chicken liver with Madeira.

❋

Stufato d'agnello alla campidanesi

LAMB STEW WITH LEMON AND GARLIC FROM CAMPIDANO

Raffaele Atzeni of the Enoteca Cagliaritana in Cagliari, on Sardinia, sent this recipe for lamb stew. Although he only sells wine and liquors and lacks kitchen facilities, he wanted me to have this recipe, one of his favorites and named for Campidano, a region near Cagliari. So how could I not include it here? In Sardinian dialect, this dish is called angioneddu a cassola. *The terra-cotta* cassola, *a traditional cooking pot, is derived from the Spanish* cazuela, *as Spaniards ruled Sardinia at one time. Some versions of the recipe omit the onions, but this stew is almost identical to the Spanish* cochifrito *of lamb served in the Rioja region, except for the absence of* pimentón *(paprika). Serve the stew with roast potatoes.*

Serves 6

Olive oil for sautéing

3 pounds lamb shoulder, trimmed of excess fat and cut into 2-inch pieces

3 onions, thickly sliced

4 cloves garlic, minced

½ cup dry white wine

1 cup meat stock, or as needed

¼ cup fresh lemon juice, or to taste

Salt and freshly ground black pepper

Preheat the oven to 350°F.

Warm a few tablespoons of olive oil in a sauté pan over high heat. Add the lamb, in batches, and brown quickly on all sides. Using a slotted spoon, transfer to a *cassola* or ovenproof braising pan and set aside.

Warm a few tablespoons of olive oil in a sauté pan over medium heat. Add the onions and sauté briefly to begin to soften. Add the garlic and sauté for a minute or two. Add the onions and garlic to the lamb. Then add the white wine and enough stock just to cover the meat.

Cover and bake until the lamb is tender, about 1½ hours. Remove from the oven, stir in the lemon juice to taste, and season with salt and pepper. Serve hot.

MATCHING POINTER: *This lamb stew is as well suited to whites as it is to bold rosés or medium-bodied reds. Play up the herbal notes in the selection. The lemon, white wine, and garlic will benefit from this additional flavor nuance.* ❋ **ITALIAN WINES:** VERMENTINO (SARDINIA), PINOT NERO ROSATO (LOMBARDY) ❋ **ALTERNATIVE WINES:** SAUVIGNON BLANC, ESPECIALLY SANCERRE AND POUILLY-FUMÉ FROM FRANCE, "VIN GRIS" OF PINOT NOIR (FRANCE, CALIFORNIA)

Aristà di maiale alla fiorentina

FLORENTINE ROAST PORK LOIN

In Italy, the pork is so sweet and tender that this excellent Florentine roast
carries an intense flavor. American pork is blander and leaner, however, and dries out easily,
so I advise brining the meat for a few days before roasting, to keep it moist and juicy.
If you are serving the roast warm, simple roast potatoes or olive oil mashed potatoes and bitter
greens such as Swiss chard, dandelion, or broccoli rabe are ideal accompaniments to balance
the richness of the meat. At Enoteca Baldi in Panzano, in the heart of Chianti country near the
town of Radda, I was served the sliced roast at room temperature, accompanied with
peperonata, a dish of sauteed sweet red and yellow peppers. You may also dress the cold pork
with a thin emulsified dressing of Dijon mustard, balsamic vinegar, and olive oil.
Slices of leftover aristà *make a great sandwich, too.*

Serves 6

BRINE:

½ cup sugar

½ cup kosher salt

1 cup hot water

12 juniper berries, bruised

6 allspice berries, bruised

2 bay leaves

2 teaspoons dried thyme

12 coriander seeds

2 teaspoons white or black peppercorns, bruised

¼ cup fresh rosemary leaves

6 cups cold water, or as needed

1 bone-in pork loin roast, 4 to 5 pounds

6 cloves garlic

4 tablespoons fresh rosemary leaves

Salt and freshly ground black pepper

Pinch of ground cloves

To make the brine, select a deep, nonreactive pan large enough to hold the pork. Combine the sugar, salt, and hot water in a large pitcher and stir until the sugar and salt are dissolved. Add all of the spices and herbs and the 6 cups cold water and stir well. Let cool completely.

Place the pork loin in the pan and pour the brine over the loin. Make sure the pork is covered by the liquid. If it is not, add cold water as needed to cover. Cover and refrigerate for 2 days.

Preheat the oven to 450°F.

Remove the pork from the brine and wipe dry. Sliver 3 of the garlic cloves and insert the slivers and 2 tablespoons of the rosemary leaves into the slits between the bones. Finely mince the remaining 3 garlic cloves and 2 tablespoons rosemary. Combine with salt and pepper to taste and the ground cloves and rub this paste all over the roast. Put the pork in a roasting pan.

Roast the pork until an instant-read thermometer inserted into the thickest part of the roast away from the bone registers 145°F, 45 to 60 minutes. Remove from the oven and let the roast rest for 15 minutes, or until you can handle it comfortably, then remove the meat in one piece from the bones. Using a sharp knife, cut into slices ½ inch thick and arrange on a platter. (Of course, if you like, you can keep the meat on the bone and cut it into chops.) Serve warm or at room temperature.

MATCHING POINTER: *The accompanying selection of side dishes (peppers versus mashed potatoes and greens) is as critical in matching this pork recipe with wine as the pork itself. The brine supplies a savory edge, especially between the varied sweet spices and the salt. Bright red regional selections seem made in heaven.* ❊ **ITALIAN WINES:** ROSSO DI MONTALCINO, REGULAR (NOT RISERVA) CHIANTI CLASSICO ❊ **ALTERNATIVE WINES:** SANGIOVESE (CALIFORNIA), BEAUJOLAIS-VILLAGES

La padellaccia

PORK AND BORLOTTI BEAN STEW

*Renzo Franceschini is the knowledgeable and passionate sommelier of the
Enoteca Vino Vino in Terni. He and his wife, Paola, opened their enoteca twenty years ago
in a building that was once an ancient pharmacy, in the historic center of this
charming Umbrian town. Umbria is known for its pork dishes, roast suckling pig, and succulent
sausages. In his letter, Renzo explained that the kinds of foods to which he is attracted are
in harmony with the rhythms of nature and are also linked with ancient peasant traditions,
some of them tied to pre-Christian and early Christian religious festivals. I'm a pushover
for dishes that have a long history, too, so I was most interested in la padellaccia (the wicked
pan), a rustic stew of beans and pork. Renzo serves the stew in January, after a winter
festival at which a pig is slaughtered. It is hearty cold-weather fare and a perfect dish for
serving with a glass of the local vino da tavola. While the spirit of Umbria is "fat is good,"
you might want to serve some braised greens with this dish, as it is quite rich.*

<u>Serves 8</u>

2 cups (about 1 pound) dried borlotti beans

2 quarts water

2½ teaspoons salt

6 to 8 cloves garlic, minced

Needles from 1 fresh rosemary sprig, chopped (about 2 tablespoons)

1 teaspoon freshly ground black pepper, plus pepper to taste

½ to 1 teaspoon red pepper flakes

4 tablespoons extra-virgin olive oil

3 pounds boneless pork shoulder or butt, cut into 1½-inch pieces

Juice of 1 large lemon

Grated pecorino cheese

To cook the beans, pick them over, rinse well, place in a bowl with water to
cover generously, and soak overnight. The next day, drain the beans and place in a
saucepan with the 2 quarts water. Bring to a boil over medium-high heat, reduce

the heat to low, cover, and simmer until tender but not soft, about 40 minutes. Add 1 teaspoon of the salt during the last 15 minutes of cooking. Remove from the heat and set aside.

Combine the garlic, rosemary, the remaining 1½ teaspoons salt, the 1 teaspoon pepper, and red pepper flakes to taste in a bowl. Heat the olive oil in a large sauté pan over high heat. Add the pork pieces, in batches, and stir until golden, 8 to 10 minutes. Sprinkle the browned meat with the garlic mixture and the lemon juice and stir well to coat with the spices. Reduce the heat to low, cover, and cook until the meat is tender, 45 to 60 minutes. According to the original recipe, while the meat cooks, you must keep "draining the fat as it accumulates in the pan and reserving it." Most pork sold in the United States today is quite lean, however, and does not give off much fat, so keep whatever it does give off in the pan with the meat. If the meat seems dry or starts to stick, add a bit of water or stock.

If when the pork is done, there is extra fat in the pan, spoon it into a large saucepan and use it to warm the cooked beans. Otherwise reheat the beans over low heat in their own liquid. Transfer the beans to a large serving dish and sprinkle with lots of black pepper and pecorino cheese. Spoon the pork over the beans and serve. Alternatively, combine the pork and beans in a pot and heat together to serving temperature, then transfer to a serving dish and sprinkle with the pepper and cheese. Serve the stew hot or warm.

Note: Borlotti beans are similar to cranberry beans. If you can't find either of them, use cannellini beans. You may want to add a chopped onion or two to the beans while they simmer.

MATCHING POINTER: *Slow braises of meat (especially white meat) preclude the automatic reaction to serve a red. The rosemary and garlic send one in search of a wine of rustic character, while the consistency of slow-cooked meat and beans suggests a selection of some weight.* ❊ **ITALIAN WINES:** RISERVA OR REGULAR TORGIANO ROSSO, ORVIETO CLASSICO ❊ **ALTERNATIVE WINES:** MERLOT (FRANCE, NEW ZEALAND), UNOAKED AND EARTHY CHARDONNAY

❋

Polpette al barese

LITTLE PORK MEATBALLS FROM BARI

*Italians loyally support their local businesses with pride. The Enoteca De Candia
has been in operation in the Apulian city of Bari for seventy-five years. During World War II
it doubled as a bomb shelter. Despite its long history, the owners have never gotten around
to adding a full kitchen. This did not stop Alessandra De Candia from generously sending me
many traditional Apulian recipes. These pork-and-cheese meatballs were among them. They may
be served hot as a small plate, all golden and crunchy, without a sauce. Or they may be
incorporated into a* ragù *to dress pasta or lasagna. I particularly like them in a tomato sauce
with greens. Accompany with polenta or olive oil mashed potatoes.*

<u>Serves 6</u>

1 pound ground meat, part veal and part pork or all pork

1 cup fresh bread crumbs, soaked in broth, milk, or water, then squeezed dry

⅔ cup grated pecorino cheese

6 tablespoons chopped fresh flat-leaf parsley

2 or 3 cloves garlic, minced

1 or 2 eggs, lightly beaten

Salt and freshly ground black pepper

Olive oil for frying

OPTIONAL GREENS:

2 pounds spinach or Swiss chard, large stems removed

2 tablespoons olive oil

1½ cups chopped onion

2 cloves garlic, minced

1 cup Tomato Sauce (page 69)

1 cup meat stock

1 teaspoon grated lemon zest

Salt and freshly ground black pepper

To make the meatballs, combine the meat, bread crumbs, cheese, parsley, and garlic in a bowl. Mix in 1 egg. If the mixture seems dry, add the second egg. Season with salt and pepper. Fry a nugget of the mixture to test the seasoning. When you are happy with the flavors, form the mixture into walnut-sized balls.

Pour olive oil to the depth of ¼ inch into a large sauté pan and place over high heat. When the oil is hot, add the meatballs and fry, turning as necessary, until golden on the outside. If you are serving them plain, continue frying them until cooked through, about 10 minutes, then turn out onto a plate. If you are combining them with the greens, remove from the heat.

If serving with greens, rinse the greens well, then place in a large sauté pan with only the rinsing water clinging to the leaves. Place over medium heat and cook, turning as needed, until wilted, 3 to 5 minutes. Transfer to a colander and drain well, pressing with the back of a spoon. Chop coarsely, squeeze dry, and set aside.

Warm the olive oil in a large sauté pan over medium heat. Add the onion and garlic and sauté until tender, about 10 minutes. Add the Tomato Sauce, stock, and lemon zest and bring to a simmer. Add the browned meatballs and simmer for several minutes until cooked through. Add the cooked greens and simmer for a minute or two longer until heated through. Taste and adjust the seasoning, then serve hot or warm.

MATCHING POINTER: *Medium-bodied red wines with a trace of earth and adequate tannins (to balance the bitterness from the greens) are a good match.* ❄ **ITALIAN WINES:** ROSSO CONERO, NEBBIOLO D'ALBA   ❄   **ALTERNATIVE WINES:** GRENACHE BLENDS (SOUTHERN FRANCE, NORTH AFRICA, SPAIN), PINOT NOIR (CALIFORNIA'S CENTRAL COAST, BURGUNDY)

✳

Carpaccio alla bagna cauda

RAW BEEF WITH OLIVE OIL, GARLIC, AND ANCHOVY

On first glance, you might think that this recipe is an example of
Italian fusion: a Venetian meat creation topped with a Piedmontese sauce. The reality
is that carne cruda, *chopped or sliced raw beef, has long been a part of the Piedmontese kitchen.*
Dressed simply with olive oil and a squeeze of lemon, it is sometimes topped with
shavings of white truffles, a regional addiction. Carpaccio, however, was created at
Harry's Bar in Venice in 1950, the year of a major exhibition of the works of famed Venetian
painter Vittore Carpaccio, whose paintings adorn the local church of San Giorgio degli
Schiavoni. Legend has it that the dish was whipped up for a frequent customer whose doctor
had placed her on a diet forbidding cooked meat. Now traditional carne cruda *is*
commonly known by the more modern "carpaccio."

Carpaccio is a natural for the enoteca menu. The sliced meat is typically
refrigerated between sheets of oiled parchment or plastic wrap; then when an order is placed,
the meat is slapped onto a serving plate and garnished in innumerable ways. Entire carpaccio
menus have been created with the beef as a base for thin slices of porcini or raw artichokes
or shavings of Parmesan. At the Enoteca del Gatto in Anzio, the beef is topped with
toasted pine nuts, Parmesan curls, and a drop or two of aged balsamic vinegar.

While Harry's Bar serves carpaccio with a mayonnaise-based sauce, L'Enoteca Les Pertzes,
a wine bar in Cogne in Val d'Aosta, serves a carpaccio of young veal topped with bagna cauda.
Bagna cauda, a Piedmontese specialty, is associated with the garlic-loving province of Cuneo.
It is a hot sauce of olive oil, garlic, and anchovy into which diners typically dip pieces of bread
or grissini *and vegetables such as carrots, celery, cardoons, red peppers, and mushrooms.*
But it is also a delicious topping for raw beef, as this recipe illustrates.

Serves 6

1½ pounds high-quality beef or veal fillet or lean baby beef

6 large fresh mushrooms, thinly sliced (optional)

3 baby artichokes, sliced paper-thin (optional)

Freshly ground black pepper

BAGNA CAUDA:

½ cup extra-virgin olive oil

16 to 24 cloves garlic, any green sprouts removed, minced

4 ounces olive oil–packed anchovy fillets, finely chopped

¼ cup unsalted butter

The quality of the meat is of primary importance, so it is imperative to patronize a top-quality butcher. Ask the butcher to slice the meat paper-thin. Some recipes recommend freezing the meat and then slicing it, but I find that the thawed meat tastes rather watery. As an alternative, ask the butcher to slice the meat about ⅓ inch thick, and then you can pound it to the desired thinness between sheets of plastic wrap or oiled parchment paper.

To prepare the *bagna cauda,* combine the olive oil, garlic, and anchovies in a small pan and warm over very, very low heat, stirring often and mashing the anchovies with a wooden spoon, until you have a creamy sauce, about 15 minutes. Add the butter and stir until the butter melts. Keep warm.

To serve the carpaccio, place the sliced beef or veal on 6 plates. If the slices are small, arrange them in an overlapping rose pattern. If they are large, use one or two to cover each plate. If desired, top the meat with the mushrooms and artichokes, then grind on a little black pepper. Drizzle the *bagna cauda* over the meat and serve.

MATCHING POINTERS: *Here, the meat is unimportant to the match. The powerful personality of the* bagna cauda *drives the pairing, and since the anchovies and garlic are the critical elements, you can pour a white. If going red, keep your tannins in check.* ❄ **ITALIAN WINES:** VALTELLINA OR COMPARABLE RED, VERNACCIA DI SAN GIMIGNANO OR COMPARABLE WHITE ❄ **ALTERNATIVE WINES:** RUEDA (SPAIN), LIGHT-OAK-AGED HERBAL MERLOT

✳

Carne salata

SPICE-AND-SALT-CURED BEEF

*A specialty of the Trentino and Alto Adige, carne salata is traditionally cured in
a salt brine with herbs and spices, then served in very thin slices, like carpaccio. You will find it
in the Enoteca Alois Lageder in Bolzano, the Enoteca Gastronomia Franzelli in Bressanone,
and the Enoteca del Ristorante Boivin in Levico. This recipe is an approximation of carne salata
and produces a truly voluptuous dish. Although beef fillet is expensive, the yield is excellent
and the cooking time minimal. Once it is seared, the beef stores well in the refrigerator
for about 5 days. While it does require some minor tending for 8 days, I think you will find
the results more than worth the few minutes required each day.*

Serves 10 to 12

2 tablespoons brown sugar

2 teaspoons chopped fresh thyme

¼ teaspoon ground cloves

½ teaspoon ground ginger

½ teaspoon ground allspice

½ teaspoon ground mace or freshly grated nutmeg

2 tablespoons freshly ground black pepper

1 teaspoon coriander seeds, toasted and ground

1 whole beef fillet, about 5 pounds, trimmed of all fat and sinews (about 3 pounds
after trimming)

2 tablespoons kosher salt

Horseradish sauce (page 106)

In a small bowl, stir together the sugar, thyme, and all of the spices except the salt.
Rub the fillet with the spice mixture and place it on a nonreactive platter. Cover
with aluminum foil and refrigerate for 2 days. After 2 days, rub the fillet with the
salt and refrigerate for 8 more days. Turn the meat once a day.

Prepare a fire in a charcoal grill, preheat a broiler, or heat a stove-top griddle pan
or heavy sauté pan over medium-high heat. Sear the beef fillet, turning as needed,

on all sides until an instant-read thermometer inserted into the thickest part registers 90°F.

Let the meat cool completely, then slice thinly. Serve drizzled with the horseradish sauce or accompanied with a salad of bitter greens and beets dressed with extra-virgin olive oil and topped with shavings of Parmesan or ricotta salata cheese.

MATCHING POINTER: *This delicious, if not exotic, beef dish is well matched with juicy reds, piquant and peppery, or rich and aromatic whites. Take into consideration a similar spice character (Alsace, Germany, Austria, northeast Italy). To ensure the white wine affinity, cook the beef more rather than less.* ❋ **ITALIAN WINES:** TEROLDEGO (TRENTINO), TRAMINER/GEWÜRZRAMINER (NORTHEAST) ❋ **ALTERNATIVE WINES:** PINOT NOIR (OREGON, CALIFORNIA), GEWÜRZTRAMINER (ALSACE, GERMANY)

❋

Polpettone alla romana
ROMAN MEAT LOAF

Polpettone is the Monday special at Enoteca Corsi on the via del Gesù in Rome, but it's an everyday affair at Bottega del Vino di Anacleto Bleve on the via Santa Maria del Pianto, the major shopping street in the Roman ghetto. With its cozy dining room and walls lined with cases of wine, this popular wine bar, run by Anacleto Bleve, is always packed at lunch. A refrigerated display cabinet holds the assorted salads, and a blackboard menu announces the daily specials. The meat loaf can be served warm or at room temperature. It also can be used on top of bruschetta. At Bottega Bleve, it is often paired with a plate of concia, sautéed zucchini dressed with a bit of lemon juice and chopped mint.

Serves 6

1 pound ground beef
¾ cup fresh bread crumbs, soaked in beef stock or water, then squeezed dry
¼ cup chopped fresh flat-leaf parsley
2 or 3 cloves garlic, minced
½ cup grated onion (optional)
1 or 2 raw eggs, lightly beaten

Salt and freshly ground black pepper

Freshly grated nutmeg (optional)

3 hard-boiled eggs, peeled

½ cup diced roasted bell peppers

2 cups Tomato Sauce, (page 69)

Preheat the oven to 350°F.

In a bowl, combine the beef, bread crumbs, parsley, garlic, and the onion, if using. Mix in 1 raw egg; if the mixture is too dry, add the second raw egg. Season with the salt, pepper, and the nutmeg, if using. Fry a nugget of the mixture to test the seasoning.

Form half of the mixture into a rectangle and place in an oiled baking pan. Make an indentation lengthwise down the center, and place the hard-boiled eggs in a row in the indentation. Distribute the diced peppers over the eggs. Cover the eggs with the remaining ground meat mixture, encasing them fully. If desired, brush the top with a bit of the sauce.

Bake until cooked through, when tested with a knife, about 1¼ hours. Remove from the oven and let rest for 10 minutes. Meanwhile, reheat the sauce. Cut the meat loaf into thick slices and serve with the warm sauce. You can also serve the meat loaf at room temperature with or without the sauce.

MATCHING POINTER: Such a homey dish is best paired with a red wine of similar character, a bit coarse and easy to enjoy. The rich consistency of meat loaf pairs well with a full-bodied selection with ample weight. The tomato sauce demands some acid (sharpness), while the eggs, which mitigate all wine qualities, give permission for a wine of impressive personality. ❊ **ITALIAN WINES:** AGLIANICO DEL VULTURE, AMARONE ❊ **ALTERNATIVE WINES:** CARIGNANE BLENDS, ZINFANDEL

✳

Tagliata di manzo al Brunello di Montalcino
SLICED STEAK WITH WINE SAUCE

Tagliata di manzo *probably originated in Tuscany, home of the famous* bistecca
alla fiorentina, *but it is now one of the most popular dishes throughout Italy. It may be served warm or at room temperature accompanied with classic Tuscan white beans or atop a bed of greens. Giovanni Rotti of Enoteca Giovanni in Montecatini Terme serves a fine* tagliata *marinated in a premium wine. The quality of the wine comes as no surprise, as the* signore *boasts a wine list of over five hundred labels. He takes immense pride in his Tuscan kitchen, and he's not one to skimp on ingredients. His marinated steak is seared rare and served with reduced pan juices made with an aged Brunello and aromatics. Sautéed spinach is a suitable accompaniment.*

<u>Serves 4 to 6</u>

3 whole cloves

½ small cinnamon stick

2 bay leaves

1 clove garlic

2 fresh sage leaves

1 fresh rosemary sprig

1 whole beef fillet or thick T-bone or porterhouse steak, about 2½ pounds

½ carrot, peeled and chopped

½ celery stalk, chopped

1 onion, chopped

½ bottle 7- or 8-year-old Brunello di Montalcino

2 tablespoons olive oil, plus more for sautéing

Beurre manié made from 3 tablespoons each unsalted butter and all-purpose flour

Salt and freshly ground black pepper

Put the cloves, cinnamon stick, bay leaves, garlic, sage, and rosemary on a square of cheesecloth, bring the corners together, and tie securely. Place the meat, carrot, celery, onion, and cheesecloth pouch in a nonreactive container, pour in the wine, turn the beef to coat evenly, cover, and refrigerate for 24 hours.

The next day, remove the beef and cheesecloth pouch and set aside. Strain the vegetables, reserving the wine and vegetables separately.

Warm the 2 tablespoons olive oil in a medium saucepan over medium heat. Add the vegetables and sauté until golden, about 15 minutes. Add the reserved wine and cheesecloth pouch, reduce the heat to low, and simmer for 1 hour.

Pass the contents of the pan through a food mill placed over a clean pan, then place the pan over low heat. Work together the butter and flour for the *beurre manié*, and gradually whisk it into the sauce to thicken. Season with salt and pepper and remove from the heat. Keep warm.

Pat the meat dry. Pour enough olive oil into a large sauté pan to form a film on the bottom and place over high heat. Sear the beef on all sides, 4 to 5 minutes on each side. It should still be quite rare but hot all the way through. Transfer to a cutting board and cut into slices about ¼ inch thick. Arrange on a platter and spoon the warm sauce over the top.

Florentine Tagliata Variation: Rub a thick steak (2½ to 3 inches) with salt, coarsely ground black pepper, and extra-virgin olive oil. (Although not traditional, you may want to add a few chopped fresh herbs, such as rosemary or thyme, to the salt and pepper.) Grill or sear on the stove top, slice, and serve atop a bed of arugula, shaved Parmesan, and a drizzle of extra-virgin olive oil. Place a lemon alongside.

MATCHING POINTER: *While this dish suggests a brawny Brunello, any rich and broad-shouldered red wine will work fine. Sticking with the Sangiovese grape (the Brunello base) is recommended, although similar-styled red wines will suffice. The more cooked you like your meat, the younger your wine should be.* ❋ **ITALIAN WINES:** BRUNELLO DI MONTALCINO, SUPER TUSCAN SANGIOVESE AND/OR CABERNET-BASED BLEND ❋ **ALTERNATIVE WINES:** RICH AND SPICY ZINFANDEL, CABERNET SAUVIGNON

Petto d'anatra all'aceto balsamico ed arancia

DUCK BREAST WITH BALSAMIC VINEGAR AND ORANGE

Sliced duck breast dressed with balsamic vinegar and orange is a menu standard at Il Simposio, at the Enoteca Costantini in Rome, and at the Enoteca del Ristorante Bidin in Lignano Sabbiadoro, run by brothers Luigino and Mario Bidin. It is also one of the top-selling plates at Enoteca Frascati, in the wine town of Frascati, outside of Rome. The latter is run by Slow Food members Paola Buglia, Paola Busi, Piera D'Onorio, and Fabrizio Ippolito, who took five small rooms in a Risorgimento palazzo and created a most simpatico environment for wine and food. The cooked duck breasts can be eaten warm, but they are usually served at room temperature.

<u>Serves 2</u>

2 Muscovy duck breast halves, about ½ pound each

Salt and freshly ground black pepper

Pinch of ground cinnamon (optional)

3 tablespoons aged balsamic vinegar

¼ cup fresh orange juice

Grated zest of 1 orange

Extra-virgin olive oil for dressing greens (optional)

Mixed greens such as arugula, watercress, and mâche (optional)

Orange sections (optional)

Preheat the oven to 450°F.

Using a sharp knife, score the skin of the duck breasts in a crosshatch pattern, but do not cut into the meat. Rub the duck breasts with salt and pepper and a bit of cinnamon, if you like.

Heat a large ovenproof sauté pan over medium heat. Place the duck breasts, skin side down, in the pan and cook until they render their fat, about 8 minutes. Drain off the fat from the pan and slip it into the oven for about 8 minutes for medium-rare. (You may instead finish the breasts on top of the stove, turning them over and sautéing for 5 to 8 minutes longer.)

Transfer the duck breasts to a cutting board. Return the pan to medium-high heat, add the vinegar, orange juice, and orange zest and deglaze the pan, scraping up the browned bits on the pan bottom. Slice the duck breasts on the diagonal, arrange on a serving plate, and spoon the pan juices over them.

If you want to serve the duck in a salad, combine the pan juices with a little olive oil to form a vinaigrette. Arrange the sliced duck over a bed of greens and drizzle with the vinaigrette. You may also add orange sections as a garnish.

MATCHING POINTER: *Duck is best with rich-textured wines. While one can attempt to cut the richness with high acidity, matching rich body with rich body seems wiser. The orange juice and zest and balsamic vinegar contribute sharp-sweet notes that match well with exotic whites or jammy reds.* ✳ **ITALIAN WINES:** BARBERA D'ALBA, DRY MOSCATO GIALLO (FRIULI, NORTHEAST) ✳ **ALTERNATIVE WINES:** PINOT NOIR (ESPECIALLY CALIFORNIA'S CARNEROS AND RUSSIAN RIVER BASIN), VIOGNIER, PARTICULARLY CONDRIEU

✳

Galletto ripieno
STUFFED CHICKEN BREAST

> *Once your friends know your obsessions, they do their best to feed the fire.*
> *My friend Don Frediani knew I was interested in enotecas, so after he visited the Enoteca*
> *La Torre in Viterbo, in the region of Lazio, he wrote that he was highly impressed*
> *with the place. He loved his meal at the enoteca and couldn't resist sending me his*
> *interpretation of* galletto ripieno, *a dish he ate that day. The chicken was stuffed with a*
> *local green called* pan di zucchero, *but endive or frisée works beautifully as well.*

<u>*Serves 8 as a tasting portion, 4 for dinner*</u>

4 whole chicken breasts, about 1 pound each, boned, halved, and skinned
Salt and freshly ground black pepper
6 heads Belgian endive or frisée, parboiled (5 to 8 minutes for endive, 3 to 5 minutes for frisée), refreshed in ice water, and drained
1 small bunch broccoli rabe, parboiled for 2 to 3 minutes, drained, and chopped
Olive oil for brushing and sautéing

1 onion, finely chopped

2 celery stalks, finely chopped

2 carrots, peeled and finely chopped

Chicken stock to cover

½ lemon

Preheat a broiler, or prepare a fire in a grill.

Place each chicken breast half between sheets of plastic wrap and pound until thin. Sprinkle with salt and pepper.

Trim the tough bases of the endive or frisée heads. Cut 4 of the heads in half lengthwise, and place a half on each breast. Roll up and tie with kitchen string. Chop the remaining endive or frisée and set aside with the broccoli rabe. Brush the rolled chicken breasts with olive oil and sprinkle with salt and pepper.

Place the rolled breasts on a broiler pan or grill rack and broil or grill, turning as necessary, until browned and cooked through but still moist, 8 to 10 minutes. Set the cooked chicken aside.

Meanwhile, pour enough olive oil into a sauté pan to form a thin film on the bottom and place over medium heat. Add the onion, celery, and carrots and sauté until soft and pale gold, 15 to 20 minutes. Add the broccoli rabe, the chopped endive or frisée, and enough chicken stock just to cover. Simmer until the vegetables are very soft, about 15 minutes. Transfer the contents of the pan to a blender or food processor and purée until smooth. Taste and adjust the seasoning. Add a squeeze of lemon, if desired.

Remove the strings from the chicken breasts and cut crosswise into slices about ½ inch thick. Reheat the sauce. Spread the warm sauce on a serving platter or individual plates, and place the warm or room-temperature sliced chicken on top of the sauce.

MATCHING POINTER: *The bitter greens are as essential to selecting the wine here as the chicken itself. Indeed, chicken is a relative blank canvas on which one adds "flavor" and "texture" with wine. Bitter means tannic, so keep that in mind. Very pungent whites can harmonize nicely also.* ❋
ITALIAN WINES: COLLI AMERINI ROSSO OR SIMILAR MEDIUM-BODIED RED, FRASCATI OR COMPARABLE LOCAL WHITE ❋ **ALTERNATIVE WINES:** CABERNET SAUVIGNON BLENDS (SOUTH AMERICA), SAUVIGNON BLANC (FRANCE, NEW ZEALAND)

Rollata di vitello

STUFFED VEAL ROLL

*When I lived in Rome, my butcher used to prepare stuffed veal legs in this manner.
I later discovered that this was not a specialty of Lazio but of Piedmont. It is an ideal dish
for an enoteca, as the slices of rolled veal can be served warm or at room temperature.
In Ferrara, the filling might be a thin omelet, sliced mortadella and prosciutto (or cooked
chopped spinach), another omelet, and then another layer of prosciutto. In the south,
these rolled legs are usually called* braciole *and are stuffed with ground meat, fennel sausage
meat, strips of provolone, and hard-boiled eggs and are braised in tomato sauce and wine.*

<u>Serves 6 to 8</u>

1 leg of veal, 4 pounds, butterflied

About 6 prosciutto slices (not too thin)

6 mortadella slices

Freshly grated nutmeg

2 or 3 cloves garlic, slivered

About 3 fresh rosemary sprigs

Salt and freshly ground black pepper

2 tablespoons unsalted butter

2 tablespoons olive oil

2 large onions, cut into ¼-inch cubes (2½ to 3 cups)

6 carrots, peeled and cut into ¼-inch cubes (about ¾ cup)

4 celery stalks, cut into ¼-inch cubes (about ¾ cup)

About 2 cups dry white wine, or as needed to cover

About 2 cups chicken or veal stock, or as needed to cover

Open up the veal leg and remove the visible gristle and any excess tendons and fat.
Arrange the slices of prosciutto and mortadella on the leg. Sprinkle with a few
generous gratings of nutmeg. Roll up and tie with kitchen string. Cut slits in the
veal and insert a few garlic slivers into them. Slip the rosemary sprigs under the
string, and sprinkle the roast with salt and pepper and a few more gratings of nutmeg.

Warm the butter and olive oil in a heavy braising pan over high heat, and brown the veal on all sides. Add the onions, carrots, and celery, then pour in the wine and stock to cover. (The amount of wine and stock you will need depends on the dimensions of your braising pan.) Gradually bring the liquid to a gentle boil, reduce the heat to low, cover, and simmer until the veal is tender when pierced and an instant-read thermometer inserted into the thickest part of the leg registers 130°F. This should take about 1½ hours.

Transfer the veal leg to a platter and let rest until warm or at room temperature. Remove the strings and discard. Cut the leg into slices about ⅓ inch thick and arrange attractively on a platter.

MATCHING POINTER: *The selection of prosciutto and mortadella in the filling suggests a wine with spicy notes. A basic red, peppery and redolent of red fruit, will best show off the dish. If serving at room temperature or even chilled, play up the fruit in the wine and think about the possibility of rosé.* ❈ **ITALIAN WINES:** TAURASI, VINO NOBILE DI MONTEPULCIANO ❈ **ALTERNATIVE WINES:** GIGONDAS OR OTHER SOUTHERN RHÔNE RED, PERIQUITA OR DÃO (PORTUGAL)

Vitello tonnato/Veal in Tuna Sauce: An ideal plate for enotecas such as N'Ombra de Vin in Milano, Enoteca Migliori in Ascoli Piceno, and Enoteca Corsi in Rome. Braise an unstuffed rolled veal leg as above. Reserve the pan juices. Chill the veal. To serve, remove the strings, slice thin, and top with the Tuna Sauce, below.

Salsa di tonno/Tuna Sauce: Combine reserved ¼ cup veal stock, 2 egg yolks, 6 ounces oil–packed tuna, 4 chopped anchovy fillets, 4 tablespoons lemon juice, and 2 tablespoons wine vinegar in a food processor. Process to a smooth purée, then gradually beat in 1 cup olive oil until the sauce emulsifies. Season with salt and pepper. Spoon this sauce over the sliced veal and sprinkle with parsley and capers.

MATCHING POINTER: *This dish eludes the classic wine and food dictums as it pairs veal (which is independently wine neutral) with tuna, which can go easily with red or white. Indeed, locally they recommend and pair rosé, which plays to both and is a good choice. A more ample white that has high acidity, or a sharper red (of lighter body/structure) will be quite good.* ❈ **ITALIAN WINES:** PINOT NERO ROSATO (FRANCIACORTA), BARDOLINO CHIARETTO ❈ **ALTERNATIVE WINES:** ROSÉ BLENDS (FRANCE, SPAIN), PINOT BLANC (CALIFORNIA, OTHER NEW WORLD)

Verdure
VEGETABLES

Pitta di patate POTATO PIE FROM APULIA

Asparagi in salsa ASPARAGUS WITH HARD-BOILED EGG SAUCE

Funghi trifolati SAUTÉED MUSHROOMS

Radicchio all'aceto balsamico e pancetta croccante
RADICCHIO WITH BALSAMIC VINAIGRETTE AND PANCETTA

Finocchio e indivia gratinato FENNEL AND ENDIVE GRATIN

Peperonata SWEET PEPPER RAGOUT

Melanzana alla parmigiana BAKED EGGPLANT PARMESAN

left: *Asparagi in salsa*
ASPARAGUS WITH HARD-BOILED EGG SAUCE, page 145

Verdure

VEGETABLES

AT AN ENOTECA, many of the *piatti del giorno* feature seasonal vegetables. These are precooked and served hot in gratins or at room temperature, dressed simply with extra-virgin olive oil and lemon, or with a citrus- or herb-infused oil. *Verdure sott'olio di casa* are vegetables marinated in oil and herbs, put up in the enoteca kitchen or purchased from specialty producers. These are often for sale at the *dispensa* area of the enoteca, along with condiments and preserves, honeys, olive oils, and other regional specialties.

Asparagus becomes a festive plate when served with chopped hard-boiled eggs and your choice of oil or vinegar. *Funghi trifolati*, sautéed mushrooms, are most flavorful when warm and may be used as a topping for *bruschetta* or as a sauce for polenta or gnocchi. Sautéed zucchini or peppers are ideal at room temperature, usually accompanying platters of cooked meat or spread atop slices of grilled bread.

Baked eggplant gratin, baked radicchio dressed with a warm pancetta and balsamic vinaigrette, fennel and endive gratin, and *pitta di patate*, an Apulian potato pie, are easy to reheat in individual portions in the oven.

Pitta di patate

POTATO PIE FROM APULIA

A savory cake made from mashed potatoes is found on menus throughout Italy. In the north, it is called tortino di patate. *In Naples, it is often known as* gattò di patate, *from* gâteau, *the French word for cake, as in the past many wealthy Neapolitans employed a French chef, called a* monzu *in dialect, after the word* monsieur. *Elsewhere in the south, the same cake is sometimes dubbed a* pitta, *meaning "pie." The cake may be layered and stuffed, or the mashed potatoes may be topped as if a pizza crust. This is an ideal enoteca dish, as it takes to reheating beautifully and is a perfect neutral foil for a glass of white wine.*

<u>Serves 6</u>

1⅓ cups diced coarse country bread (crusts removed)

¼ cup unsalted butter, melted, or olive oil

½ teaspoon salt, plus salt to taste

¼ teaspoon freshly ground black pepper, plus pepper to taste

2½ to 3 pounds russet potatoes if baking or Yukon Gold potatoes if boiling

½ cup all-purpose flour

¾ cup grated pecorino cheese

2 eggs, lightly beaten

½ cup milk, or as needed

FILLING:

¼ cup extra-virgin olive oil, plus more for drizzling

2 onions (about 1 pound), sliced

6 large tomatoes, peeled, seeded, and diced

¼ cup capers, rinsed and drained

6 tablespoons pitted black olives, coarsely chopped

First, make the bread crumbs: Preheat the oven to 350°F. Pulse the bread cubes in a food processor until you have fine crumbs. Spread the crumbs on a baking sheet. Evenly drizzle with the butter or oil and sprinkle with the ½ teaspoon salt and

¼ teaspoon pepper. Toss well to coat. Bake, stirring occasionally, until golden, about 20 minutes. Remove from the oven and measure out ⅔ cup of the crumbs. Reserve any leftover crumbs for another use.

If using baking potatoes, preheat the oven to 425°F. Prick the skin in a few places with a fork. Place on a baking sheet and bake until tender, about 1 hour. If using boiling potatoes, peel them and place in a saucepan with salted water to cover. Bring to a boil and boil until tender, 20 to 30 minutes. Drain well.

While the potatoes are still hot, pass them through a ricer placed over a bowl, first scooping the baked potatoes from their skins. Knead in the flour and pecorino cheese, then add the eggs and enough milk to make a soft dough. Season abundantly with salt and pepper. Set aside.

Preheat the oven to 400°F.

To make the filling, heat the ¼ cup olive oil in a large sauté pan over medium heat. Add the onions and sauté until tender, about 15 minutes. Add the tomatoes and cook, stirring occasionally, until they break down, about 15 minutes longer. Stir in the capers and olives and remove from the heat. Set aside.

Oil a 10-by-7-by-2-inch baking dish and sprinkle the bottom with half of the bread crumbs. Place half of the potatoes in the pan, patting them down to form an even layer. Spread the onion mixture over the potato layer. Top with the remaining potatoes, again patting down to form an even layer. Drizzle with olive oil and top with the remaining bread crumbs.

Bake until golden, about 35 minutes. Serve warm or at room temperature, cut into squares or rectangles.

MATCHING POINTER: Potatoes, while adding consistency and some sweetness, are a blank canvas for wine. Here's a perfect recipe for showing off a lovely Chardonnay or similarly rich and subtle white. Reds, even the mildest, knock out the subtle flavor of the dish.
❋ **ITALIAN WINES:** CHARDONNAY BLENDS (FRIULI, TUSCANY), VERNACCIA DI SAN GIMIGNANO ❋
ALTERNATIVE WINES: CHARDONNAY (ANYWHERE), SÉMILLON BLENDS (AUSTRALIA)

Asparagi in salsa

ASPARAGUS WITH HARD-BOILED EGG SAUCE

In the Veneto, white asparagus is an obsession. Come spring, everyone goes crazy over the fat, tender stalks. They appear on the menu every day in every restaurant, trattoria, osteria, and home until the season is officially declared over on June 13, the Feast of Saint Anthony. I first tasted this dish at the Enoteca Regionale La Serenissima in Gradisca. The kitchen uses asparagus from the nearby town of Tavagnacco, outside of Udine in Friuli. Tavagnacco is home to a giant agricultural co-op that grows only asparagus and hosts a white asparagus festival during the last two weeks in May. The best-known white asparagus in the Veneto comes from Bassano, which is also famous for its pottery. You can also try this recipe with chubby stalks of green asparagus, but they are not as sweet as the white ones.

There is no specific recipe for the sauce, as the diner makes it at the table, to suit his or her palate. Platters of cooked asparagus are passed, followed by a plate of hard-boiled eggs, cruets of olive oils from diverse regions of Italy, assorted vinegars, and salt and pepper. One scoops up a pile of asparagus and puts it on a plate. Then he or she takes a couple of eggs and mashes them with oil and vinegar to make a sauce. The stalks of asparagus are then dipped in the sauce and eaten with the fingers (always my favorite way to eat asparagus).

Allow ⅓ to ½ pound fat asparagus spears, preferably white, per person
Fresh lemon juice and sugar, if using white asparagus
2 eggs per person
Mild red wine vinegar or balsamic vinegar
Extra-virgin olive oil
Salt and freshly ground black pepper

Remove the tough ends of the asparagus spears. Using a vegetable peeler, peel the stalks to within about 2 inches of the tips if using green spears. White asparagus must be peeled completely, or they will taste bitter.

Bring a wide saucepan filled with salted water to a boil. Add the asparagus and boil until tender, 5 to 8 minutes, depending on the thickness. For white asparagus, add a bit of lemon juice and sugar to the water. Drain well, refresh in cold water, and drain again. Pat the spears dry and arrange on a platter or individual serving plates.

In a saucepan, combine the eggs with water to cover, bring to a gentle boil, and boil for 8 to 9 minutes, so that the yolks are still a bit soft in the center. Run under cold water until cool, then peel.

Each diner mashes the eggs with a fork, stirs in 1 to 2 tablespoons vinegar, adds olive oil until the consistency is saucelike, and seasons the sauce with salt and pepper. Finally, diners dip asparagus spears into their handmade sauce and eat them.

MATCHING POINTER: *Two of the hardest foods to pair with wine are asparagus and cooked eggs, so you need to overpower them with sharpness (acidity) and personality. Big whites are best, but some reds can work well, too. Remember, the odds are against you if you choose a balanced wine, so err on the sharp side.* ❋ **ITALIAN WINES:** TOCAI FRIULANO, SAUVIGNON/PINOT BIANCO (FRIULI, ALTO ADIGE) ❋ **ALTERNATIVE WINES:** CABERNET FRANC (ESPECIALLY CHINON FROM FRANCE), SAUVIGNON BLANC (FRANCE, NEW ZEALAND, CALIFORNIA)

❋

Funghi trifolati
SAUTÉED MUSHROOMS

When porcini are in season, I want to eat them every day. Sautéed, grilled, al forno, or in a torta or pasta sauce, they are meaty, earthy, and superb. In Tuscany, they are seasoned with an herb called nepitella (calamint in English), which is related in flavor to mint. It is a classic marriage. Fortunately, thanks to a friend, Don Frediani, I have a flourishing patch of nepitella in my garden, so I am able to replicate this superb Tuscan combination. Every once in awhile, fresh porcini appear at my market. The rest of the time I use a mixture of portobellos, cremini, chanterelles, and other wild mushrooms to make this dish. To enhance its flavor, I add a small amount of dried porcini. Serve funghi trifolati as they do at the Bar Shelter in Gallarate, just outside of Milan, as a little ragout on top of soft polenta or polenta crostini (page 102) or spread on grilled bread. They are also an ideal sauce for gnocchi.

Small handful (about ½ ounce) dried porcini mushrooms

5 tablespoons olive oil or equal parts unsalted butter and olive oil

1 tablespoon minced garlic

¼ cup diced pancetta or prosciutto (optional)

2 tablespoons chopped fresh *nepitella* or fresh mint, or equal parts chopped fresh mint and oregano

1 pound mixed fresh mushrooms (see recipe introduction), sliced ¼ inch thick

¼ cup dry white wine, if needed

¼ cup chopped fresh flat-leaf parsley

Salt and freshly ground black pepper

Combine the dried porcini with hot water to cover in a bowl for 30 minutes. Drain, reserving the liquid. Chop the porcini finely and set aside. Pass the liquid through a cheesecloth-lined sieve and reserve.

Warm the olive oil or olive oil and butter in a large sauté pan over medium heat. Add the garlic and pancetta or prosciutto, if using, and sauté for 2 minutes. Raise the heat to high, add half of the *nepitella* or mint (or mint and oregano) and the mushrooms, and cook quickly until tender, 6 to 8 minutes. If the mushrooms have not given off much liquid, add the wine and cook quickly until the wine is absorbed. Add the chopped dried porcini along with the strained liquid and the remaining herbs. Stir well, sprinkle with salt and pepper, and heat through. Serve at once.

Note: When I do find fresh porcini, I cut off the stems, stud the caps with thin slivers of garlic, and then marinate them in olive oil; chopped fresh herbs such as mint, winter savory, and parsley; and salt and freshly ground black pepper. I grill or broil them until tender, basting them with the scented olive oil from the marinade. When watching your budget, portobellos can stand in for the porcini.

MATCHING POINTER: *Mushrooms of all shapes, sizes, and flavors are wine foods. The more pungent the mushroom, the more likely you'll want to stay red, especially Merlot. Chanterelles like rich whites, as do shiitakes and oyster mushrooms.* ❋ **ITALIAN WINES:** POMINO ROSSO, MERLOT (VENETO) ❋ **ALTERNATIVE WINES:** MERLOT (SOUTHWEST FRANCE, WASHINGTON STATE), PINOT NOIR (FRANCE, NEW ZEALAND)

＊

Radicchio all'aceto balsamico e pancetta croccante

RADICCHIO WITH BALSAMIC VINAIGRETTE AND PANCETTA

*Balsamic vinegar, because it has been mellowed by years of aging in wood
casks, is not highly acidic and therefore does not overpower a glass of fine wine. Here,
heads of radicchio are blanched ahead of time, then put under the broiler or baked in a hot oven,
where they are basted with a little olive oil mixed with an aged balsamic. They can be served
at this point, or they can be dressed with a warm vinaigrette* con pancetta croccante, *as
they are at Enoteca La Dispensa near Mantua, in Lombardy. Sometimes the baked radicchio
is wrapped in prosciutto and dressed with balsamic vinegar, which is the case at the Osteria
del Vicolo Nuovo in Imola, in Emilia-Romagna, and at the Enoteca Frascati,
in the wine region outside of Rome.*

<u>Serves 4</u>

4 small heads radicchio
¼ cup extra-virgin olive oil
2 tablespoons aged balsamic vinegar
Salt and freshly ground black pepper

VINAIGRETTE:
5 ounces pancetta, sliced ¼ inch thick, then cut crosswise into ¼-inch-wide strips
¾ cup olive oil
2 or 3 tablespoons balsamic vinegar
Salt and freshly ground black pepper

Preheat the broiler.

Bring a large pot of salted water to a boil. Drop the radicchio into the boiling water
and cook for 2 minutes. Push them under the water, as they have a tendency to
bounce up. Drain well and squeeze out excess moisture carefully. If they are large,
cut them in half lengthwise.

In a small cup, whisk together the olive oil and balsamic vinegar.

Place the radicchio on a broiler pan and sprinkle with salt and pepper. Brush with some of the olive oil and vinegar. Broil for 3 minutes, then turn and brush with more oil and vinegar and broil for 3 minutes longer. The radicchio should be golden and tender. Arrange on a platter and keep warm.

To make the vinaigrette, cook the pancetta in a small saucepan or sauté pan over medium heat until the pancetta has rendered its fat and is slightly crisp, about 5 minutes. Add the olive oil and vinegar and season with salt and pepper. Spoon this over the cooked radicchio. Serve hot.

MATCHING POINTER: *Radicchio is special when it comes to wine. It is often best with sharp whites (especially when raw) or equally sharp reds. Generally, austere is preferred, as its bitter edge demands attention. The balsamic will amplify that need, while the pancetta softens and buffers the angles a little and may steer you red.* ❖ **ITALIAN WINES:** YOUNG, VIBRANT FRASCATI, FREISA (ASTI, CHIERI) ❖ **ALTERNATIVE WINES:** RUEDA (SPAIN), BEAUJOLAIS

❊

Finocchio e indivia gratinato
FENNEL AND ENDIVE GRATIN

The Osteria/Enoteca Re Tarquinia in Lazio serves a dish much like this one. While you could make the succulent gratin with just fennel or just endive, they are especially harmonious together, as the sweetness of the fennel contrasts nicely with the slightly bitter quality of the endive. You can grill the endives rather than braising them. Grilling adds a smokiness that works well with the cheese, but you might not want to light the fire unless you are using it for something else as well. The mild Gorgonzola cheese labeled dolcelatte makes a wonderful topping, but equal amounts of grated Parmesan and Fontina can be substituted. Just be aware that the use of any cheese brings added salt to the dish, so be careful when seasoning. The gratin can be fully assembled ahead of time, refrigerated, and then brought to room temperature before baking.

<u>Serves 4</u>

2 large or 4 small bulbs fennel
2 large or 4 small heads Belgian endive

4 tablespoons extra-virgin olive oil or unsalted butter
Salt and freshly ground black pepper
About 1 cup water or vegetable or chicken stock
1 cup (about 5 ounces) crumbled Gorgonzola *dolcelatte* cheese
Toasted bread crumbs for dusting (optional; see Apulian Potato Pie, page 143)

Cut the fennel into quarters lengthwise and remove the central cores. Trim away any bruised outer leaves. If the bulbs are very large, cut them into eighths. Cut the endives in half lengthwise, but keep the stem end intact on each half. Preheat the oven to 450°F, or preheat the broiler.

Warm 2 tablespoons of the olive oil or butter in a sauté pan over medium heat. Add the fennel and cook, turning as needed, until golden, 5 to 8 minutes. Season lightly with salt and pepper, then add about ½ cup of the water or stock and cover the pan. Cook until very tender, about 10 minutes. Transfer to a plate and set aside.

Warm the remaining 2 tablespoons olive oil or butter in the same sauté pan over medium heat. Add the endive and cook, turning as needed, until golden, 5 to 8 minutes. Season lightly with salt and pepper, then add ½ cup the remaining water or stock and cover the pan. Cook until very tender, about 8 minutes. Remove from the heat.

Combine the endive and fennel in a large gratin dish or 4 individual dishes. (If broiling, be sure to use a flameproof dish or dishes.) Sprinkle with pepper and top evenly with the crumbled cheese. Sprinkle with a dusting of bread crumbs, if desired. Bake until the cheese is melted, 6 to 8 minutes. Alternatively, slip under the broiler until golden and bubbly, just a few minutes. Serve at once.

MATCHING POINTER: *The juxtaposition of the sweetness of cooked fennel against the sharpness of endive is challenging. The surrounding elements (stock and cheese) mitigate the harder edges. White seems the best choice.* ❊ **ITALIAN WINES:** VERMENTINO (SARDINIA), FIANO DI AVELLINO ❊ **ALTERNATIVE WINES:** CHARDONNAY (ESPECIALLY FRENCH CÔTE CHALONNAISE), PINOT GRIS (OREGON, ALSACE)

Peperonata
SWEET PEPPER RAGOUT

Peperonata *is a typical southern Italian dish, yet it was served to me at the*
Enoteca Baldi in Panzano, in Tuscany, as an accompaniment to a platter of roast pork.
While geographically unrelated, they tasted wonderful together. Red and yellow peppers are
most commonly used, but if you can't find yellow, use green. Some versions add tomato, others
not. Some add a splash of vinegar at the end of cooking, others add sugar and vinegar for
an agrodolce, *or sweet-and-sour taste. Just be careful not to add an overpowering amount of*
vinegar, as it will fight the wine. Almonds and raisins can be added as well, but keep the wine
in mind again and don't make the mixture too sweet. Peperonata *is best at room temperature.*
It is an excellent topping for bruschetta *and, when warmed, makes a great*
sauce for pasta or sautéed chicken breasts.

<u>*Serves 6 to 8*</u>

3 large red bell peppers

3 large yellow or green bell peppers

½ cup olive oil

1 or 2 onions, sliced ¼ inch thick

2 cloves garlic, finely minced

3 vine-ripened tomatoes, peeled, seeded, and diced

2 to 3 tablespoons red wine vinegar

2 tablespoons sugar (optional)

¼ cup sliced almonds, toasted (optional)

¼ cup raisins, plumped in hot water and drained (optional)

Salt and freshly ground black pepper

Cut each bell pepper in half and remove the seeds and thick ribs, then slice lengthwise about ⅓ inch wide. Warm the olive oil in a large sauté pan over medium heat. Add the onions and sauté until softened, about 8 minutes. Add the peppers and garlic, reduce the heat to low, cover, and cook until tender, about 20 minutes.

Add the tomatoes and the vinegar to taste and stir well. Then add the sugar, almonds, and/or raisins, if using. Season with salt and pepper. Simmer for a few minutes to allow the flavors to mellow and mingle. Serve warm or at room temperature.

MATCHING POINTER: *While peppers in general possess a tangy, bitter edge, usually lending themselves to red more than white, cooking softens them up. If you add the almonds and raisins, select a fruitier example. Without them, a full-flavored white or zippy young red is good.* ❖ **ITALIAN WINES:** DOLCETTO D'ALBA, ROSSO DI MONTALCINO ❖ **ALTERNATIVE WINES:** RIOJA *SIN CRIANZA* OR SIMILAR SPANISH TEMPRANILLO WINE, UNOAKED CHARDONNAY (FRANCE)

Melanzana alla parmigiana

BAKED EGGPLANT PARMESAN

*It may seem odd, but the dish that most of us call eggplant Parmesan
has very little to do with the town of Parma. In the classic southern Italian version,
most popular in Italo-American restaurants, eggplant is fried, layered with tomato sauce
and slices of mozzarella and caciocavallo cheese, and sometimes slices of hard-boiled egg,
and then topped with bread crumbs and grated pecorino or Parmesan cheese. It can be rather
heavy. I was served a delicious light version of the dish at Tuscany's popular Enoteca Baldi
in Panzano, proving that regional barriers are coming down. The eggplant took on a melting
quality after it was reheated. This gratin is ideal for entertaining, as it can be assembled
ahead of time and baked just before serving.*

<u>Serves 6</u>

3 medium-sized globe eggplants, about ¾ pound each

Salt

Olive oil for frying

2 cups peeled, seeded, and diced tomatoes

2 cloves garlic, minced (optional)

Salt and freshly ground black pepper

¾ cup grated Parmesan cheese

1½ cups fine dried bread crumbs (see note)

Peel the eggplants and slice crosswise about ⅓ inch thick. Place the slices in 1 or
2 colanders, sprinkling them with salt. Let drain for 30 minutes. Rinse and pat dry.

Preheat the oven to 400°F. Oil a baking dish that will accommodate the eggplant
slices in 2 layers.

Pour olive oil to a depth of ¼ inch into a large sauté pan, preferably nonstick, and
place over medium-high heat. When the oil is hot, add the eggplant slices, in batches,
and fry, turning once, until golden and tender, then transfer to paper towels to drain.
Add oil to the pan only as necessary to prevent sticking, or the porous eggplant will
drink more than it needs. The frying should take about 6 minutes for each batch.

To the oil remaining in the pan, add the tomatoes and cook until they break down and acquire a saucelike consistency, about 10 minutes. Add the garlic during the last 2 minutes. Season with salt and pepper.

Spread a thin layer of the tomato sauce in the prepared baking dish. Add half of the eggplant slices, then half of the remaining tomato sauce. Top with the remaining eggplant and then the remaining sauce. Scatter the grated cheese and then the bread crumbs evenly over the surface.

Bake the eggplant until the top is golden, about 25 minutes. Let rest for 15 minutes before serving.

<u>Note</u>: For a dish more southern Italy in style, add thin slices of mozzarella cheese between the layers of eggplant slices and sauce, but do not omit the bread crumb and parmesan topping. You can also make fresh bread crumbs and toast them in the oven to use for the topping. See page 99 for directions on preparing the crumbs.

MATCHING POINTER: *The texture of this preparation demands a wine of ample body. Eggplant, even when cooked, often has a bitter edge that is best countered by the tannins and peppery flavors in red wine. Sangiovese is perfect here, but many other options in the same vein exist.* ❋ **ITALIAN WINES:** BARBERA D'ASTI, CARMIGNANO ❋ **ALTERNATIVE WINES:** SYRAH BLENDS (FRANCE, CALIFORNIA), PINOTAGE (SOUTH AFRICA)

Formaggi e condimenti e confetture per formaggi

CHEESES, CONDIMENTS, AND PRESERVES

Caciù all'argentiera **FRIED CHEESE, SILVERSMITH'S STYLE**

Frico **CHEESE CRISP FROM FRIULI**

Crema di formaggio **HERBED CHEESE SPREAD**

Tomino dorato **GOLDEN GOAT CHEESE**

Fonduta piemontese **CHEESE FONDUE FROM PIEDMONT**

Ricotta infornata **BAKED RICOTTA**

Picci **STUFFED FIGS WITH BAY AND FENNEL**

Salsa di prugne all'arancia e pepe nero
PRUNE SAUCE WITH ORANGE AND BLACK PEPPER

Salame di ficchi **FIG SALAMI**

Confettura di pomodori verdi **GREEN TOMATO CONSERVE**

left: *Frico*
CHEESE CRISP FROM FRIULI, page 164

Formaggi e condimenti e confetture per formaggi
CHEESES, CONDIMENTS, AND PRESERVES

CHEESE IS THE MOST VERSATILE PLAYER on the enoteca menu. It can be a savory course in itself; part of a salad; an ingredient in a torta, focaccia, or *pizzetta*; or a garnish for soup, pasta, or vegetable gratin. It can be a filling for a dessert tart or cake, or the basis of a creamy custard or pudding. Cheese with sweet or savory accompaniments can be a perfect lunch. A *vasoio di formaggio*, a tray of assorted cheeses with fruit, bread, and condiments, is also the ideal finale after sampling many small plates. Certainly the enoteca is the perfect place to taste local cheeses at their optimum. And if ever there was a food made for wine, it is cheese.

The enoteca cook puts cheese at the heart of many dishes. Among them are *crema di formaggio,* a custom-mixed herbed cheese spread; *ricotta infornata,* a ramekin of baked ricotta for spreading on bread; and *fonduta piemontese,* a rich cheese fondue for dipping bread or vegetables or for spooning over polenta or gnocchi as a sauce. A disk of soft *robiola* might be sauced with a warm zucchini purée, and aged *montasio* or Asiago cheese is the basis for a crispy Friulian cheese cup, or *frico,* that can hold a salad, soft polenta, or cooked vegetables. In Sicily, fried *caciocavallo* cheese, anointed with oregano and lemon, is a stellar cheese plate. And *tomino,* a marinated fresh goat cheese, may be dipped in bread crumbs and sautéed or baked and served with a salad or with boiled potatoes for dipping in the melting cheese.

Cheese can also be a salad component. Sliced mushrooms may be combined with Fontina, fennel, and bitter greens. *Ovoli* mushrooms, bright orange-capped late-summer or fall fungi, are sliced thin and tossed with shavings of Parmesan, or sliced porcini are paired with *toma di Murazzano*. Goat cheese may be served warm on a bed of greens or atop a salad of peppers and red onions. Fruit and cheese are classic salad pairings: pears and *pecorino di Fossa* are tossed with arugula, and endive, apple, and walnuts are matched with a *crottin tartufo d'Alba*. All of these salads go nicely with wine if the dressing is not too tart and vinegary. Try citrus juices or a good balsamic vinegar, along with the very best olive oil you can find. Many salads are also dressed with only olive oil or a citrus-infused oil.

ASSEMBLING A CHEESE TRAY

Italians take their cheeses seriously. Therefore, the largest segment of the enoteca menu is the *vasoio di formaggio*, or cheese tray. Assorted cheeses are served with a selection of appropriate condiments. The selection might range from soft, mild, or young cheeses to hard, strong, or aged cheeses. There are the *formaggi italiani*, or Italian cheeses, and the *selezione francese*, or French cheeses. Sometimes a plate of only assorted *formaggi di capra*, goat cheeses, or *formaggi erborinati*, herbed cheeses, is offered. Red wine drinkers often want the *formaggi paste dure*, or assorted hard cheeses. There is even the *formaggi grande sapore*, the stinky cheese plate. Finally, there may be *formaggi dolci*, a sweet cheese assortment with *mascarpone*, fresh mozzarella, and Gorgonzola *dolcelatte* paired with honey, chestnut jam, fruit preserves, or slices of ripe fruit.

CHEESES WITH FRUITS AND CONDIMENTS

I'll never forget my first formal Italian cheese-tasting experience. At Enoteca Il Simposio in Rome, I ordered six "local" cheeses, three soft, two semiripe, and one aged and dry, served on a plate with a dollop of chestnut purée, some green tomato conserve, a slice of fresh pear, and a slice of a "salami" made of dried figs. I mixed and matched textures and tastes and sipped wonderful wine selected by the sommelier, Dario. I could close my eyes, and taste the food, and decide which pairings I preferred.

Pairing cheese with fruits and condiments is an art. Ripe pears, tart crisp apples, and fragrant persimmons go well with creamy and semifirm cheeses. A compote of apples cooked in red wine can make a slice of Asiago shine. Dried dates and figs, or a fig salami (page 173) with nuts, pair well with an aged goat cheese or a sliver of aged pecorino or Parmesan. Preserved walnuts or warm toasted nuts are good with Gorgonzola and a glass of port or Amarone. Aged Gorgonzola is traditionally paired with herb- or truffle-infused honeys or bitter honeys from Sardinia and a glass of *vin santo* or sweet Marsala. Look for specialty honeys at your local farmers' market, or try imported products such as wild chicory honey from Daniele DeValle in Piedmont, chestnut honey from Badia a Coltibuono in Tuscany, or honeysuckle honey from Giuseppe Coniglio in Sicily. Creamy *robiola* or *mascarpone* is sublime when paired with sweetened chestnut purée or candied chestnuts, or with prune purée, wine-soaked prunes, or nut-stuffed prunes. You can make your own spread by combining equal parts *mascarpone*, ricotta, and mild fresh goat cheese, and serve it with dark honey or lemon or orange marmalade.

A number of excellent preserves and preserved fruits are being imported as well. Look for fig, apricot, and rosehip preserves from L'Antica Drogheria in Florence, and delicious fruit preserves, candied chestnuts, and sweetened chestnut purée from the Piedmont firm Agrimontana, in Borgo San Dolmazzo. La Nicchia, from Pantelleria off Sicily, produces fine lemon marmalade and a sweet grape jam. Calabrian fig preserves and sweet grape jam are being shipped under the label Artibel. *Cotognata*, quince paste infused with cinnamon or citron, is a specialty of Apulia, but you can

find many Spanish imports as well, sold under the name *membrillo*. Apulian pear, quince, and fig pastes from the Azienda Agricola Marzano in San Pietro in Vernotico, near Brindisi, are made from only fruit, sugar, and pectin, and they are delicious.

If you'd like to try making a few condiments of your own, I have included recipes for stuffed figs, a dried fig salami for slicing paper-thin, a prune sauce spiked with orange and black pepper, and a green tomato conserve that can be sweet or savory.

WINE AND CHEESE PAIRING
Here are some suggestions from Italian sommeliers for cheese and wine pairings. Some cheeses go well with both reds and whites.

Match mild Gorgonzola with Dolcetto, and an aged Gorgonzola with Amarone or Patriglione from Taurino or with Sauternes. *Crescenza* goes well with a young Barbera.

Parmigiano-reggiano is great with a glass of Prosecco, *brut spumante* from Franciacorta, or Champagne. It also pairs smoothly with big red wines such as Chianti, Cabernet, Carmignano, and Nebbiolo. Try Asiago with a glass of Amarone or with a sparkling wine.

Fontina complements young, fruity reds such as Grignolino, Freisa, Pinot Nero, or Dolcetto d'Alba, a white wine such as Arneis, or a spicy Traminer from Friuli. Creamy *monte veronese* or *stracchino* will work with a Soave or a sparkling

Trebbiano. *Fiore sardo* can shine with a red such as Barbaresco or a *moscato passito*. *Castelmagno* is enhanced by a *moscato passito* or a Barbaresco or a Brunello. *Toma* and fresh mozzarella are nice with a Chardonnay from Friuli.

As soon as you add fruit, the balance changes. A pairing of Gorgonzola and bitter honey is served with Marsala or *vin santo*. Add fig purée and you might want to pour *vin santo*, Torcolato, or Sauternes. This is the time to be most creative. Play with the cheese, the condiments, and the wines until you achieve the taste combinations you like. It is the ultimate enoteca experience.

ITALIAN CHEESES

As a member of Slow Food, I ardently support our local (American) cheese artisans, but as a cheese fanatic, I also love Italian cheeses. Many fine examples are at our markets and cheese shops. This list of favorites has been compiled from assorted enoteca menus.

ASIAGO: Large, round cow's milk cheese, aged 3 to 9 months, from Friuli.

BRA: Cow's milk cheese from Piedmont.

BRINATA: Soft ripened sheep's milk cheese from Tuscany.

CACIOCAVALLO: Aged pear-shaped *pasta filata* (stretched curd) cow's milk cheese from Sicily.

CAPRINO: Small goat's milk cheese from Piedmont.

CASTELMAGNO STAGIONATO: Cow's milk cheese, aged from 2 to 5 months, from Piedmont.

CROTONESE: Medium-bodied, slightly sharp sheep's milk cheese, aged 6 months, from Crotone in Calabria.

FIORE SARDO: Sharp, full-flavored sheep's milk cheese from Sardinia.

FONTINA (VAL D'AOSTA): Cow's milk cheese, aged 3 to 6 months; large wheel can weigh as much as 40 pounds.

GORGONZOLA: The milder *dolcelatte* (sweet and young) and sharper aged blue-veined cow's milk cheese from Lombardy.

GRANA PADANO: Hard, granular cow's milk cheese from Lombardy, in 55- to 85-pound giant wheels.

MASCARPONE: A buttery, rich cow's milk cream cheese.

MONTASIO: Cow's milk cheese, aged 3 to 18 months, from Friuli.

MONTE VERONESE: Very smooth and creamy cow's milk cheese from Verona.

MOZZARELLA: Soft, moist, round *pasta filata* (stretched curd) cheese; the best are made from the milk of water buffaloes, but most are made from cow's milk.

PARMIGIANO-REGGIANO: The premier cow's milk cheese, aged 18 to 24 months, from Emilia-Romagna, in wheels weighing between 60 and 70 pounds; the best are made between April and November.

PECORINO DI FOSSA: Cave-aged sheep's milk cheese, aged 4 months, from Tuscany.

PECORINO ROMANO: Aged sheep's milk cheese from Lazio.

PECORINO SARDE: Sheep's milk cheese, aged 2 months, from Sardinia.

PECORINO STAGIONATO TOSCANO or **SENESE:** Aged semihard sheep's milk cheese from Tuscany.

PROVOLONE: *Pasta filata* (stretched curd) cow's milk cheese, aged 3 to 6 months, from Campania and Basilicata.

RAGUSANO: Hard cheese, salted and sometimes smoked, from Sicily.

RASCHERA: Smooth, buttery cow's milk cheese with a natural rind, from Lombardy and Emilia-Romagna.

RICOTTA: Fresh, soft sheep's or cow's milk cheese made from whey (more a dairy product than a cheese).

RICOTTA AFFUMICATA: Smoked ricotta from Calabria.

RICOTTA SALATA: Salty sheep's or cow's milk cheese from Calabria; can be shaved or grated.

ROBIOLA: Soft, round goat's or sheep's milk cheese, or a combination, aged 2 months, from Piedmont.

SCAMORZA: *Pasta filata* (stretched curd) cow's milk cheese, sometimes smoked, made throughout southern Italy.

SOTTO CENERE TARTUFATO: Semisoft cow's milk cheese blended with truffles and aged in ashes, from the Veneto.

STRACCHINO: Soft, runny, creamy cheese, related to *crescenza* cheese from Lombardy.

TALEGGIO: Semisoft washed-rind cow's milk cheese, aged 2 months, from Lombardy; often eaten at the end of the meal with fruit or preserves.

TOMA: Hard cow's milk cheese produced in the alpine regions of Piedmont and Lombardy.

TOMINO: Small fresh cow's or goat's milk cheese, usually preserved in olive oil.

UBRIACO DEL PIAVE: Sweet cow's milk cheese bathed in red wine must, from the Veneto.

Caciù all'argentiera

FRIED CHEESE, SILVERSMITH'S STYLE

Argentiera *refers to the apocryphal silversmith who prepares this dish. The title is, of course, ironic, because when people are poor, they cannot afford meat and instead have to fry cheese. The dish is a specialty of Palermo and resembles Greek* saganaki. *Given the crosscultural food exchange throughout the Mediterranean due to colonization and conquest, it is likely that the Greeks introduced this notion of fried cheese to the Sicilians.* Caciocavallo (caciù) *and provolone are ideal cheeses, as they melt but do not fall apart.*

Serves 4 to 6

1½ to 2 pounds *caciocavallo* or provolone cheese, cut into ½-inch-thick slices
All-purpose flour for dusting (optional)
Olive oil for frying
1 or 2 cloves garlic, smashed
Salt and freshly ground black pepper
2 tablespoons dried oregano
1 to 2 tablespoons red wine vinegar
Coarse country bread

Lightly dust the cheese slices in flour, if desired. Pour olive oil to a depth of ¼ inch into a large nonstick sauté pan. Add the smashed garlic and warm over medium heat until sizzling. Drop in the cheese slices, a few at a time, and fry until golden on the first side, 2 to 3 minutes. Flip and fry them until golden on the second side, about 2 minutes longer. Season to taste with salt and pepper.

Using a slotted spatula, transfer the cheese to individual plates. Sprinkle with oregano and a bit of vinegar. Serve with pieces of bread to sop up the cheese.

MATCHING POINTER: *The juxtaposition of fried texture with the softness of melting cheese is sublime with sparkling wine or young whites. Look for more rusticity in your sparkling choice and an olivey-green element in your white choice.* ❋ **ITALIAN WINES:** VERDICCHIO, GRECO DI TUFO ❋ **ALTERNATIVE WINES:** CAVA OR SIMILAR SPARKLING WINE, DRY SHERRY *(FINO* AND *AMONTILLADO)*

Frico

CHEESE CRISP FROM FRIULI

The first time I ate frico *was at a cooking class in Gianna Modotti's kitchen in Udine. The rib-sticking, tasty cheese pancake was filled with a mixture of potatoes and onions, a bit heavy for my palate, plus it was time-consuming to prepare properly. Gianna expertly and carefully kept draining the fat from the rich cheese as it accumulated. Frico seemed to be a labor of love and tradition, but I doubted that I would make it once I returned home. A few days later, I went to a wine luncheon at Enoteca La Serenissima, in Gradisca. There I was served a crisp, lacy cup-shaped* frico *filled with soft white polenta topped with grated cheese, to my taste a more appealing version.*

In an enoteca, the shells are typically made ahead of time. Preparing them to order would be a nightmare. Properly done, they resemble tuile cookies, only savory rather than sweet. They hold beautifully and are easy to make. All you need is a small nonstick sauté pan, a rubber spatula, and grated aged montasio *or Asiago cheese. You can fill the shells with soft polenta (page 101) topped with grated cheese, sautéed mushrooms (page 146), or a small salad of greens, apple slices, and chopped walnuts or hazelnuts in a mild balsamic vinaigrette (page 149).*

<u>*Makes 10 to 12 crisps*</u>

1 pound *montasio* or Asiago cheese, grated

Unsalted butter, if needed

Heat a small nonstick sauté pan over medium heat. Scatter a thin layer of grated cheese over the bottom of the pan. Let it cook for a few minutes, until the fat that comes out of the cheese begins to bubble around the edges. Press with a fork, drain any excess fat, and allow to cook until golden. Flip over with a spatula, cook for a minute to set the other side, then turn onto a small bowl or custard cup to form into a bowl or cup shape. Blot with a paper towel, then set aside on paper towels to drain. Continue to repeat this process until all of the cheese is used.

Just as when making crepes, the first *frico* may stick. To prevent this, you can brush the pan with butter. After that, they will come out easily. You can also make the crisp on a seasoned griddle. Form the cheese into circles, do not crowd them, and proceed as you would for the individual pan.

MATCHING POINTER: This dish was made for sparkling wine—white, rosé, and even red frizzante. If you are not a fan of sparkling wine, zesty whites will suffice. ✻ **ITALIAN WINES:** PROSECCO, BRACHETTO D'ACQUI ✻ **ALTERNATIVE WINES:** CHAMPAGNE OR SPARKLING WINE (BRUT, ROSÉ), GRUNER VELTLINER (AUSTRIA)

✻

Crema di formaggio

HERBED CHEESE SPREAD

While you sip your glass of wine at the counter at Milan's Le Cantine Isola, your host, sommelier Luca Sarais, may offer you this unctuous cheese mixture that he makes every day. It can be spread on bread or toast, or melted over grilled vegetables. Luca recommends Gewürztraminer "Castel Turmhof" di Tiefenbrunner or a Pinot Bianco "Vorberg" della Cantina Sociale di Terlano to accompany the spread.

Makes about 1 1/2 cups

Leaves from 2 small bunches basil, preferably with small, tender leaves
Leaves from 1 small head radicchio
3 soft fresh goat cheeses, each 5 to 6 ounces
¼ cup extra-virgin olive oil, or as needed

Finely chop the basil and radicchio leaves. Place the cheeses in a bowl and mix in the chopped leaves. Stirring constantly, gradually add the oil until you have a soft, creamy spread. Serve at room temperature.

MATCHING POINTER: This lovely spread craves a zippy young white. Between the inherent herbal character and the tang from the goat cheese, any crisp, flavorful (and unoaked) example would suffice. Take a lead from residents of the Loire Valley, where goat cheese reigns supreme, and opt for a Sauvignon Blanc. ✻ **ITALIAN WINES:** SAUVIGNON (FRIULI, NORTHEAST), PINOT BIANCO ✻ **ALTERNATIVE WINES:** SAUVIGNON BLANC (LOIRE VALLEY, FRANCE, NEW ZEALAND), RUEDA (SPAIN)

✻

Tomino dorato

GOLDEN GOAT CHEESE

A tomino is a small fresh goat's or cow's milk cheese marinated in olive oil.
Baked or sautéed goat cheese in a bread-crumb crust is a texture sensation. The crunchy
outer layer paired with melting cheese contrasts beautifully with a cool salad of bitter greens.
Erberto Messinesi, at Milan's Taverna Visconti, serves his baked goat cheese with a salad
of apples and arugula. The salad dressing must be a mild mixture of extra-virgin olive oil
and an aged balsamic vinegar to avoid any conflict with the wine.

<u>Serves 1</u>

½-inch-thick slice or 1 individual fresh mild goat cheese, about 3 ounces
Extra-virgin olive oil for marinating
Generous pinch of chopped fresh thyme, sage, or marjoram (optional)
¼ cup fine dried bread crumbs or toasted bread crumbs (page 105)
1 to 2 tablespoons unsalted butter

Place the goat cheese in a shallow dish and add olive oil just to cover. Add the herb, if using, and turn the cheese to coat evenly. Cover and refrigerate for a few hours or as long as overnight.

Spread the bread crumbs on a flat plate. Lift the cheese from the marinade and dip it in the bread crumbs, coating well on both sides. Melt the butter in a small nonstick sauté pan over medium heat. Add the cheese and fry, turning once, until the crumbs are golden and the cheese is starting to soften, about 3 minutes on each side. Using a slotted spatula, transfer to a plate and serve using one of the suggestions in the introduction. Alternatively, place the crumb-coated cheese in a small oiled baking dish and bake in a preheated 400°F oven until golden and bubbling, 6 to 8 minutes.

MATCHING POINTER: The pairing of goat cheese and Sauvignon Blanc is a time-honored match. Other choices are possible, but white wines are best. Avoid large doses of oak if you plan to serve the cheese over wilted greens. ✻ **ITALIAN WINES:** SAUVIGNON BLENDS (NORTHEAST), SOAVE ✻ **ALTERNATIVE WINES:** UNOAKED OR MINIMALLY OAKED SAUVIGNON BLANC, PINOT BLANC (FRANCE)

✳

Fonduta piemontese

CHEESE FONDUE FROM PIEDMONT

*If you should find yourself in the town of Cuneo, step into Osteria della Chiocciola for
a glass of wine and a classic* fonduta piemontese. *Please don't confuse this dish with the cheese
fondue of Switzerland.* Fonduta piemontese *is made with Italian Fontina, a much creamier,
earthier cheese than the Gruyère used for the Swiss version, plus milk and egg yolks.
An even more luxurious concoction is the addition of a layer of freshly shaved white truffles.
The precious fungi are astronomically expensive, but a bit of truffle oil added after the cheese
is melted is a reasonably priced substitute. It can be a dip for pieces of toasted bread or sticks
of briefly blanched vegetables, or can serve as a sauce for gnocchi, polenta, or risotto cakes.*

Serves 2

5 ounces Fontina cheese, cut into small dice

½ cup milk

2 tablespoons unsalted butter

2 egg yolks

½ teaspoon truffle oil (optional)

If possible, combine the cheese and milk in a bowl and let soak overnight in the
refrigerator or for at least a few hours at room temperature.

Melt the butter in the top pan of a double boiler over simmering water. Add the
cheese and milk mixture. Whisk well to combine, then continue to whisk, adding
the egg yolks one at a time and whisking well after each addition. When the *fonduta*
is smooth and creamy, after about 6 to 8 minutes, stir in the truffle oil, if desired.

Serve at once in warmed bowls as a dip with one of the suggestions in the introduction.

*MATCHING POINTER: The nuttiness of the Fontina and the sweet earthiness of the truffle oil make
this a wine-friendly dish. Modest reds or earthier whites are good. A sparkling wine can be a nice,
refreshing alternative.* ✳ **ITALIAN WINES:** SPARKLING OR STILL WHITE FRANCIACORTA, GHEMME,
NEBBIOLO D'ASTI/ALBA ✳ **ALTERNATIVE WINES:** MODESTLY OAKED PINOT NOIR, CRU BEAUJOLAIS
(MORGON, MOULIN À VENT)

＊

Ricotta infornata

BAKED RICOTTA

Bergamo, in Lombardy, is divided into two parts: the modern city below and the old city, Bergamo Alto, on the hill. On the main street of the upper city, facing a majestic old palazzo with a nineteenth-century deco facade and interior, is the Vineria Cozzi, run by Simona Gotti and her husband, Roberto, who is the cook. Along with an assortment of frittatas and torte salate, he serves this timballo of ricotta. To prepare this simple condiment, you need a good fresh ricotta cheese, sweet and soft in texture.

Serves 4

2 cups (about 1 pound) ricotta cheese (see recipe introduction)
3 tablespoons chopped fresh sage or rosemary
Salt and freshly ground black pepper
Extra-virgin olive oil
Grilled or toasted coarse country bread

Preheat the oven to 300°F. Place the ricotta cheese in a bowl, stir with a fork, mix in the sage or rosemary, and season to taste with a little salt and pepper. Pack into a lightly oiled 4-cup ovenproof crock. Drizzle the top with extra-virgin olive oil.

Bake until warm and a little quivery, about 15 minutes. Serve warm with grilled or toasted bread.

MATCHING POINTER: *The irony here is that less is more. If your ricotta is especially "sweet," the wine should have more fruit. Keep the rosemary in check with a kiss of oak or an herbal flavor (think Sauvignon Blanc).* ＊ **ITALIAN WINES:** PINOT GRIGIO, CINQUE TERRE BIANCO ＊ **ALTERNATIVE WINES:** PINOT GRIS/GRIGIO (FRANCE, CALIFORNIA, OREGON), CHENIN BLANC (FRANCE, SOUTH AFRICA)

※

Picci

STUFFED FIGS WITH BAY AND FENNEL

*An ideal accompaniment for a glass of dessert wine, these stuffed figs also
go nicely with an assortment of soft and dry cheeses such as* caprino, pecorino, or
Parmigiano-reggiano. *In her book* Red, White & Greens, *Faith Heller Willinger calls these*
picci, *adds walnuts to the traditional combo, and gives Carmignano in Tuscany the nod
as their place of origin. Michele Scicolone's book* La Dolce Vita *attributes them to
the town of Bari in Apulia, calls them* ficchi barese *and uses almonds instead. To intensify
the flavor, the version from Bari warms the stuffed figs in a 350°F oven for 15 to 20 minutes.
Ideally, these should be made at least 2 weeks before you want to eat them, so start
stuffing now. They keep very well in an airtight container at room temperature.*

3 dozen dried Black Mission or Calimyrna figs
3 dozen walnut halves or unblanched almonds, toasted
2 tablespoons fennel seeds
3 dozen bay leaves

Cut a slit at the top of each fig and insert the nut of your choice along with a few
fennel seeds. Pinch closed.

Layer the figs in a crock, alternating with layers of the bay leaves. Sprinkle with any
leftover fennel seeds. Cover tightly with plastic wrap and store in a cool place for at
least a week, preferably two.

MATCHING POINTER: *Figs and wine typically form a happy partnership, and this preparation is no
exception. The dried nature of the figs suggests a "raisining" treatment in the wine's production, and
indeed* passito *wines are best. A red or rosé is preferred, but white would be lovely, too.*
※   **ITALIAN WINES:** RECIOTO DELLA VALPOLICELLA, SAGRANTINO DI MONTEFALCO PASSITO   ※
ALTERNATIVE WINES: RICH, JAMMY ZINFANDEL, YOUNG GRENACHE BLENDS (SOUTHERN FRANCE,
AUSTRALIA)

※

Salsa di prugne all'arancia e pepe nero

PRUNE SAUCE WITH ORANGE AND BLACK PEPPER

The Enoteca del Gatto in Anzio is a family affair. Franco del Gatto and his wife, Simonetta, run the enoteca along with their children, Daria and Cesare, the latter working as sommelier. The marble serving counter is the original banco di mescita *installed in 1936, when Franco's father, Cesare, opened the place as an osteria. Simonetta del Gatto makes a number of conserves to serve with cheese. I particularly liked her suggestion to serve a slightly peppery prune sauce with cheese. You might want to try making it with fresh Italian prune plums.*

<u>*Makes about 1½ cups*</u>

1 cup pitted prunes, finely chopped
½ cup water
½ cup fresh orange juice, or as needed
¼ cup sugar or honey
Grated zest of 1 orange
Fresh lemon juice (optional)
1 teaspoon fresh coarsely ground black pepper, or to taste
Slices of *robiola* cheese

Combine the prunes, water, ½ cup orange juice, sugar or honey, and orange zest in a small saucepan over medium heat. Bring to a boil, reduce the heat to low, and cook until the sauce thickens, about 20 minutes. If the mixture is too sweet, add a bit of lemon juice or more orange juice for balance, then add a nice grinding of black pepper.

Let cool, cover, and store in the refrigerator for up to 3 months. Bring to room temperature, before serving. Serve with *robiola* cheese.

MATCHING POINTER: *The distinctive sauce of this recipe longs for full-flavored reds that suggest sweetness. The orange and pepper play supporting roles, but are flavors found—and welcomed— in many wines.* ※ **ITALIAN WINES:** AMARONE, ANY *PASSITO ROSSO* ※ **ALTERNATIVE WINES:** YOUNG AND AMPLE CÔTES DU RHÔNE, SHIRAZ (AUSTRALIA)

Salame di ficchi
FIG SALAMI

This fig "salami" is a specialty of the town of Ascoli, in the Marches. It is sold at the dispensa *at Enoteca Migliori along with* mistrà, *a local anise-flavored liqueur produced by herbalist Girolomo Varnelli. The fig paste is mixed with anise liqueur and reduced grape must and sometimes with chopped walnuts. Then it is rolled into a log resembling a salami, wrapped in fig leaves, and aged for at least a month in a wooden cask. In the absence of fig leaves, aluminum foil is the less glamorous alternative.*

Makes one 15-inch-long roll

1 pound dried figs, preferably not too hard
4 tablespoons balsamic vinegar reduced by ½ over heat to a syrup
2 tablespoons anise liqueur such as Sambuca or anisette, or as needed
About ½ cup coarsely chopped walnuts (optional)

Chop the figs with a cleaver, or cut into small pieces with sharp scissors. Place in a food processor with the liquids and the nuts, if using, and pulse until the mixture clumps together. Add a bit more liquid if needed.

Turn out onto a work surface covered with aluminum foil, and shape the mixture into a log about 15 inches long. Loosely cover with foil and let the log sit at room temperature until it firms up and forms a skin, about 2 weeks. Then wrap the log in foil and store in the refrigerator for up to 3 months.

The fig paste is best after a month, as it will be firmer and thus easier to slice. Use a sharp knife dipped in hot water. Slice thin and serve with goat's or sheep's milk cheese and a few warm toasted walnuts.

MATCHING POINTER: The nuts add a bitter nuance to this recipe, while, from a wine point of view, the anise threads the entire preparation together. As with the stuffed figs, passito *or raisined wines are best.* ❋ **ITALIAN WINES:** RECIOTO DELLA VALPOLICELLA, SAGRANTINO DI MONTEFALCO PASSITO ❋ **ALTERNATIVE WINES:** RICH, JAMMY ZINFANDEL, YOUNG SYRAH BLENDS (SOUTHERN FRANCE, AUSTRALIA)

*****

Confettura di pomodori verdi
GREEN TOMATO CONSERVE

I first tasted a version of this conserve while indulging in a cheese platter at
one of my favorite wine bars, Il Simposio at the Enoteca Costantini, located on a corner of
Rome's teeming Piazza Cavour. Piero Costantini's cellar offers an astounding selection
of Italian wines, arranged by region, as well as an in-depth selection of grappas.
In Bologna, Le Fate, a combination enoteca and trattoria run by sommelier Antonella Menegatti
and Maria Rita Occhi, offers a house-made green tomato conserve for pairing with cheese.

You can take two directions with this recipe: make it tart and quite spicy to serve as an
accompaniment for cold meats such as cooked chicken or pork or mild and creamy cheeses,
or make it sweet and fragrant as an accompaniment for dessert cheese platters.

Makes 8 half-pint jars

BASIC SWEET CONSERVE:

4 pounds green or green-striped tomatoes, cored and quartered, or green cherry
    tomatoes, stems removed

2 lemons, sliced paper-thin and quartered

4 cups sugar

1 teaspoon ground cinnamon

1 teaspoon ground cloves

1 to 2 cups water

2 teaspoons vanilla extract (optional)

ADDITIONS FOR SAVORY CONSERVE:

½ to 1 pound fresh ginger, to taste, peeled and thinly sliced

1 to 2 cups vinegar

2 onions, chopped (optional)

12 large cloves garlic (optional)

12 jalapeño chiles, chopped (optional)

1 teaspoon cayenne pepper (optional)

If making a sweet conserve, put the tomatoes in a deep, wide canning kettle. (I like enamel-covered cast iron, as it retains heat well and tends not to scorch.) Add the lemon slices and sugar and let sit for a few hours for the sugar to draw some moisture out of the tomatoes. Add the cinnamon, cloves, and 1 cup of the water. Place over high heat and bring to a boil, stirring from time to time. Reduce the heat to medium and cook, stirring often and adding more water if it threatens to scorch, until the mixture thickens and registers about 220°F on a candy thermometer. This should take 20 to 30 minutes. Add the vanilla if desired.

If making a savory conserve, proceed as directed for the sweet conserve through allowing the tomatoes, lemons, and sugar to sit for a few hours. Combine the cinnamon, cloves, and ginger in a blender or food processor with about ½ cup of the vinegar and purée until smooth. Then, if desired, add the onions, garlic, jalapeños, and/or cayenne to the blender or processor along with 1 more cup of the vinegar. Purée until smooth, adding more vinegar if the mixture is too stiff. Add the purée to the tomatoes and bring to a boil over high heat, stirring from time to time. Reduce the heat to medium and cook, stirring often, until the mixture thickens and registers about 220°F on a candy thermometer. Again, this should take 20 to 30 minutes.

Ladle the conserve into hot, sterilized canning jars and seal. Process for 10 minutes in a hot-water bath. Remove from the water bath, let cool, check the seals, label, and store in a cool, dark place for up to 1 year. Alternatively, ladle into hot, sterilized jars, cap, and refrigerate for up to 3 months.

MATCHING POINTER: This conserve has two variations. If going tart, play up the sharpness in the wine and/or what you are serving. The cheese and/or cold meats will help define your selection. If going sweet, look for a dessert-styled wine with a hint of the exotic. ❀ **ITALIAN WINES:** FOR TART CONSERVE, DRY WHITE OLTREPÒ PAVESE, TREBBIANO D'ABRUZZO; FOR SWEET CONSERVE, RECIOTO DI SOAVE, ALBANA DI ROMAGNA DOLCE ❀ **ALTERNATIVE WINES:** FOR TART CONSERVE, PINOT BLANC (FRANCE, CALIFORNIA), DRY MÜLLER-THURGAU (NEW ZEALAND, GERMANY); FOR SWEET CONSERVE, BEAUMES-DE-VENISE (FRANCE), LATE-HARVEST SAUTERNES (FRANCE, CALIFORNIA)

Dolci
SWEETS

Crostata di formaggio e frutta **MASCARPONE AND FRUIT TART**

Amor polenta **CRUMBLY CORNMEAL CAKE**

Zaletti **CORNMEAL-RAISIN COOKIES**

Panna cotta alla castagne **CHESTNUT CREAM**

left: *Panna cotta alla castagne*
CHESTNUT CREAM, page 186

Dolci

SWEETS

AFTER MUNCHING ON FRIED OLIVES, cured meats, or smoked fish, most enoteca customers may have a craving for something sweet. The typical dessert menu breaks down into two categories: cheeses with sweet accompaniments and a few *dolci* that put the wine at center stage. I have made a careful but limited selection of a cookie, a cake, a tart, and a pudding that will allow the wines to sing.

Biscotti are classic partners for a glass of *vin santo,* providing crunch and a bit of sweetness at the end of a meal. I have not included a recipe for biscotti because, as you may know, good ones are easily purchased in a wide variety of styles, from baroque new-wave to macadamia to double chocolate to chocolate and sun dried cherry. But in order for the dessert wine to stand out, less is more. I prefer a simple classic with almonds or almonds and hazelnuts, with the subtle perfume of anise. As they are not easy to find here, I have given the recipe for *zaletti,* a delightful

cornmeal-raisin cookie from the Veneto, ideal for dunking as well.

I've also selected *Amor polenta* a cornmeal cake that can be served by itself or dipped in zabaglione. For the tart there's a recipe for a Roman *crostata di formaggio e frutta,* which pairs rich and creamy cheese with a layer of fruit in a pastry shell.

Puddings and custards are also harmonious with dessert wine. I particularly like the *panna cotta alla castagne,* a chestnut-enhanced version of the classic pudding, served with either persimmon or chocolate sauce.

Crostata di formaggio e frutta

MASCARPONE AND FRUIT TART

The theme of a fruit tart with a custardy cheese topping is a popular one.
In Rome, the cheese filling is poured over a layer of sour cherry jam (visciole) or brandied
cherries. (Of course, pitted fresh Bing cherries macerated in a bit of Kirsch would
be wonderful, too.) In her excellent Regional Foods of Southern Italy, *Marlena de Blasi*
gives a Roman variation in which the cheese custard is scented with cinnamon and orange
marmalade and is spread atop a layer of plumped prunes or fresh plums. I suggest that when
in Rome, we should do as the Romans do and follow the seasons. Try berries or apricots in
summer, and in late fall or winter use sliced apples or pears sautéed in butter and a bit
of sugar. A thin layer of chopped nuts may be pressed onto the crust to absorb excess
fruit juices and thus keep the crust crisp. A bit of Frangelico or Tuaca would echo
the hazelnut theme, and Amaretto would play up the almond flavor. Add a bit to the
cheese or to the crust for yet another dimension.

PASTRY:

1⅓ cups all-purpose flour

¼ cup sugar

6 tablespoons chilled unsalted butter

1 egg yolk

3 tablespoons heavy cream

1 tablespoon Frangelico, Tuaca, or Amaretto liqueur (optional)

1 tablespoon grated orange zest (optional)

¼ cup finely chopped blanched almonds (optional)

FILLING:

1½ cups *mascarpone* cheese

½ cup sugar

1 whole egg, plus 3 egg yolks

Finely minced zest of 1 orange

1 tablespoon Frangelico, Tuaca, or Amaretto liqueur (optional)

½ teaspoon ground cinnamon (optional)

Choice of one: 1½ cups raspberries or blackberries; 2 pears, peeled, cored, sliced, and sautéed in a few tablespoons unsalted butter with a little sugar until tender; about 2 cups pitted prunes, plumped in ⅓ cup dark rum or plum brandy and drained; or 1½ cups plum jam or sour cherry jam

To make the pastry, stir together the flour and sugar in a bowl. Cut in the butter with a pastry blender until the mixture resembles coarse meal. In a small bowl, whisk together the egg yolk, cream, and the liqueur and zest, if using. Incorporate the yolk mixture into the flour mixture until the dough just comes together in a rough ball. Form into a ball, wrap in plastic wrap, and chill for 1 hour.

Preheat the oven to 400°F. Have ready a 9- or 10-inch tart pan with a removable bottom.

Flatten the dough slightly and place between 2 sheets of parchment paper. Roll out into a round about 3 inches larger than the pan's diameter and ⅛ inch thick. Peel off the top sheet of parchment and carefully ease the round, paper side up, into the pan. Peel off the remaining sheet of parchment and gently press the dough against the bottom and sides of the pan. Fold over the edge of the dough to form thicker sides. If it tears, patch it with a scrap of dough. It is very forgiving. If you like, press the chopped almonds onto the bottom and sides of the dough. (If not baking immediately, place in the freezer until ready to bake.)

Line the pastry crust with aluminum foil and fill with pie weights or raw rice. Bake for 15 minutes. Remove the weights and foil, reduce the oven temperature to 350°F, and continue to bake until golden brown, 10 to 15 minutes longer. Transfer to a rack to cool.

Reduce the oven temperature to 325°F.

To make the filling, in a bowl, combine the cheese, sugar, whole egg and egg yolks, orange zest, and the liqueur and cinnamon, if using. Whisk just until well mixed. Arrange the fruit or spread the jam over the bottom of the cooled crust. Pour in the cheese custard.

Bake the tart until the custard is just set, about 25 minutes. Transfer to a rack to cool. Remove the pan sides and slide the tart onto a serving plate. Serve warm or at room temperature.

MATCHING POINTER: Mascarpone, at once tart and sweet, requires a wine selection that has some zest. The fruit will likely dictate your selection, as the nature of the berry fruit (raspberries, blackberries) is different than that of orchard fruit (pears). For the berries, select a sparkling wine, and for the peaches, a sweet white dessert wine. ❀ **ITALIAN WINES:** ASTI SPUMANTE, RECIOTO DI SOAVE ❀ **ALTERNATIVE WINES:** OFF-DRY TO DEMI-SEC (DEPENDING ON FRUIT) CHAMPAGNE OR OTHER SPARKLING WINE, SÉMILLON BLENDS (FRANCE, CALIFORNIA)

Amor polenta

CRUMBLY CORNMEAL CAKE

In Bologna, at the combination enoteca and osteria Olindo Faccioli, Carlo
Faccioli serves this delicious house-made cornmeal cake with a dollop of warm zabaglione.
The enoteca was established in 1924 by his grandfather Olindo, who bottled regional wines such
as Alban, Sangiovese, Lambrusco, and Cabernet Sauvignon. The original bancone
di mescita, the pink marble wine counter, is still in use. Carlo writes that his chef, Antonio
Franco, has lived in Bologna for over thirty years, but originally comes from Erice,
in Sicily. Naturally, he serves a Sicilian specialty, cannoli, as one of his selected desserts.
He also makes amor polenta, a Lombardian favorite that is produced commercially
in Mantua under the name torta sbrisolona, or crumbly cake. The name comes from sbriciolare,
"to crumble," because when it is cut, the edges break off into crumbs. It is an ideal
vehicle to show off a dessert wine and, for double wine heaven, to pair with zabaglione.
As Carlo didn't send the family recipe, this particular version is based on one from
I dolci della cucina regionale italiana, by Fernanda Gosetti. You may also serve the cake
with wine-poached pears, a fruit compote, berries, a cold zabaglione (see below), or plain.

1 cup (½ pound) unsalted butter, at room temperature

1¾ cups sifted confectioners' sugar, or 1 cup granulated sugar

3 whole eggs, plus 6 egg yolks, lightly beaten

½ teaspoon almond extract, or 2 tablespoons Strega liqueur

1 teaspoon vanilla extract

1⅓ cups fine-grind yellow cornmeal, sifted

1 cup all-purpose flour

2½ teaspoons baking powder

1 cup ground almonds

OPTIONAL ZABAGLIONE:

7 egg yolks

6 tablespoons sugar

1 cup sweet Marsala or other sweet dessert wine such as _moscato passito_

1 cup heavy cream

Preheat the oven to 350°F. Butter and flour a standard loaf pan or a 9-inch cake pan.

In a bowl, using an electric mixer on high speed, beat together the butter and sugar until fluffy, about 10 minutes. Gradually beat in the eggs, a little at a time, allowing each addition to be incorporated and absorbed into the butter mixture before adding more. Then mix in the almond extract or liqueur and the vanilla. In another bowl, stir together the cornmeal, flour, baking powder, and nuts. Gently fold the flour mixture into the butter mixture; do not overmix. Pour into the prepared pan.

Bake until golden and a toothpick inserted into the center of the cake emerges clean, 40 to 50 minutes. Transfer to a rack and let cool completely.

To make the zabaglione, whisk the egg yolks in a bowl until blended. Whisk in the sugar and wine and pour through a sieve into a shallow heatproof bowl. Rest the bowl over hot water in the lower pan of a double boiler or a saucepan placed over medium heat. Whisk until the custard forms a stiff trail, 10 to 15 minutes. Remove the bowl from the pan and rest it in a bowl filled with ice and water to chill. Stir it from time to time as it cools. Meanwhile, whip the cream until stiff peaks form.

When the custard is fully chilled, fold the cream into it.

To serve, unmold the cake and place it on a serving plate. Slice thinly and serve with the zabaglione, if desired.

MATCHING POINTER: *Pick up on the toasted grain aspect of this dessert. Its dry, crumbly texture makes it perfect for a sparkling wine, but it will show well against many white dessert wines, too. Finally, don't overlook fortified wines, as it is also a natural recipe for those styles.* ❖ **ITALIAN WINES:** MOSCATO LIQUOROSO, TORCOLATO (BREGANZE) ❖ **ALTERNATIVE WINES:** DEMI-SEC CHAMPAGNE, BROWN OR CREAM SHERRY

❋

Zaletti
CORNMEAL-RAISIN COOKIES

The name zaletti *is dialect, derived from the word* giallo *or "yellow." It comes from the use of yellow cornmeal in the cookie dough. According to Emilio Baldi, who operates Enoteca Vino Vino in Venice, all of the best Venetian cookies are dry and profit from being dipped in a glass of dessert wine such as Torcolato or Malvasia, or a glass of warm zabaglione.*

<u>Makes about 4 dozen cookies</u>

1¼ cups plus 1 tablespoon fine-grind yellow cornmeal
1¼ cups plus 3 tablespoons all-purpose flour
½ teaspoon salt
¾ cup unsalted butter, at room temperature
⅓ cup plus 1 tablespoon sugar
3 egg yolks
1 teaspoon vanilla extract
⅔ cup raisins, plumped in hot water

In a bowl, sift together the cornmeal, 1¼ cups plus 1 tablespoon flour, and the salt. In a large bowl, using an electric mixer, beat together the butter and sugar until fluffy. Beat in the egg yolks and vanilla. Add the flour mixture to the butter mixture

and beat until well blended. Drain the raisins and toss them in the remaining 2 tablespoons flour. Fold the raisins into the dough.

Preheat the oven to 375°F. Butter 2 baking sheets.

Divide the dough in half. Place half of the dough on a floured work surface and, using your palms, roll into a log about 8 inches long and 1½ inches in diameter. Repeat with the remaining dough. Cut the logs into rounds about ⅓ inch thick, and arrange the rounds on the prepared baking sheets, spacing them about 2 inches apart.

Bake the cookies, one sheet at a time, until pale gold, 10 to 15 minutes. Transfer to racks to cool. Store in an airtight container at room temperature for up to 2 weeks.

MATCHING POINTER: *Most of us are now familiar with the concept of dipping cookies into wine, and the automatic choice is vin santo. But look to something more youthful for these gems.* ❀ **ITALIAN WINES:** TORCOLATO, RECIOTO DI SOAVE ❀ **ALTERNATIVE WINES:** TOKAY (HUNGARY), 10-YEAR-OLD TAWNY PORT

❀

Panna cotta alla castagne
CHESTNUT CREAM

Enoteca Faraoni, a rustic and jovial wine shop–wine bar in Livorno, is owned by sommelier Paolo Faraoni. The Faraoni family has been serving wine since the early 1900s, and today they carry over one thousand labels. One of their dessert specialties is panna cotta alla castagne, *served with a sauce made from fresh persimmons. When persimmon season ends, you can be sure that no one complains if they offer the dessert with chocolate sauce, in the manner of* monte bianco.

Chestnut purée is sold in cans. Some brands are sweetened and have a bit of vanilla added. Others are unsweetened, in which case you will probably need to add about ½ cup sugar. Chestnut purée labeled confettura di castagne *is sold in jars as a spread for bread. It may be used in this recipe as well. If you use the* confettura, *you won't need to add sugar.*

<u>Serves 8</u>

1 tablespoon unflavored gelatin

¼ cup water

2 cups heavy cream

1 cup milk

1½ cups chestnut purée

1 teaspoon vanilla extract, or to taste

½ cup sugar, if chestnut purée is unsweetened

A few tablespoons dark rum, or to taste (optional)

In a small cup, sprinkle the gelatin over the water and let stand to soften for 3 to 5 minutes. Meanwhile, combine the cream and milk in a saucepan and warm over medium heat. Stir the softened gelatin into the warmed cream mixture until it dissolves. Whisk in the chestnut purée and vanilla. Add the sugar and the rum to taste, if using. (If the chestnut purée is very stiff, pulse it in a food processor with the warmed cream mixture.)

Pour into 8 custard cups or lightly oiled metal molds. Cover and refrigerate until firm, 4 hours or overnight. Unmold onto small plates and serve with persimmon purée or chocolate sauce (following).

Salsa di cacchi/Persimmon Sauce: Peel and seed 4 to 6 ripe Hachiya persimmons. Place in a blender or food processor with fresh orange juice and sugar to taste and some ground cinnamon, if you like. Process until smooth.

Salsa di cioccolata/Chocolate Sauce: Combine 8 ounces semisweet chocolate and ¾ cup light cream in a saucepan. Place over very low heat to melt, then whisk until smooth.

MATCHING POINTER: *This is a lovely match for wine, in terms of both flavor and consistency. While both are "dark" in nature, the persimmon sauce requires a fresher wine, while the chocolate opens up the opportunity for aged versions. Don't overwhelm with chocolate, or you'll lose the subtlety.* ❁
ITALIAN WINES: VIN SANTO, ALEATICO DOLCE (APULIA) ❁ **ALTERNATIVE WINES:** TOKAY (HUNGARY), MUSCAT PORT (AUSTRALIA)

BIBLIOGRAPHY

Alberini, Massimo. *Antico Cucina Veneziana.* Casale Monferrato: Piemme, 1990.

Barth, Hans. *Osteria, Guida spirituale delle osterie italiane.* Padua: Franco Muzzio Editore, 1998.

————. *La cucina romana.* Rome: Newton & Compton, 1983.

Boni, Ada. *Italian Regional Cooking.* New York: Bonanza Books, 1969.

Cunsolo, Felice. *Guida gastronomica d'Italia.* Novara: Istituto Geografica de Agostini, 1975.

de Blasi, Marlena. *Regional Foods of Southern Italy.* New York: Viking Press, 1999.

del Conte, Anna. *Gastronomy of Italy.* New York: Prentice Hall Press, 1987.

Field, Carol. *Celebrating Italy.* New York: William Morrow, 1990.

————. *Italy in Small Bites.* New York: William Morrow, 1993.

Gho, Paola, and others. *Osterie d'Italia.* Bra: Slow Food Editore, 1999.

Gosetti della Salda, Anna. *Le ricette regionale italiane.* Milan: Solares, 1967.

Gosetti, Fernanda. *I dolci della cucina regionale italiana.* Milan: Fabbri editore, 1993.

Harbutt, Juliet. *The World Encyclopedia of Cheeses.* New York: Lorenz Books, 1998.

Jenkins, Nancy Harmon. *Flavors of Puglia.* New York: Broadway Books, 1997.

————. *Flavors of Tuscany.* New York: Broadway Books, 1998.

Jenkins, Steven. *Cheese Primer.* New York: Workman Press, 1996.

Kleiman, Evan. *Cucina del Mare.* New York: William Morrow, 1993.

Kramer, Matt. *A Passion for Piedmont.* New York: William Morrow, 1997.

Lanza, Anna Tasca. *The Flavors of Sicily.* New York: Clarkson Potter, 1996.

Oldenburg, Ray. *The Great Good Place.* New York: Paragon House, 1989.

Perwanger, Hanna. *Cucina tradizionale del sud Tirolo.* Bolzano: Casa Editrice Athesia, 1992.

Plotkin, Fred. *Italy for the Gourmet Traveler.* Boston: Little, Brown and Company, 1996.

————. *Recipes from Paradise.* Boston: Little, Brown and Company, 1997.

Pradelli, Alessandro Molinari. *La cucina sarda.* Rome: Newton & Compton, 1997.

Riolo, Claudio. *Le enoteche d'Italia.* Bologna: Veronelli Editore, 1992.

Riolo, Claudio, Luciano Ferraro, and Elena Riolo. *Enoteche: Buon vino e piccolo proposte di cucina.* Milan: Alexa Edizioni, 1996.

Sassu, Antonio. *La vera cucina in Sardegna.* Rome: Casa Editrice Anthropos, 1983.

Schiaffino, Mariarosa, Monica Centanni, and Girolomo Marcelle. *Venezia in cucina.* Milan: Arnoldo Mondadori, 1994.

Scicolone, Michele. *La Dolce Vita.* New York: William Morrow, 1993.

Scott, Paolo. *Wine and Cheese of Italy.* Rome: Gremese, 1999.

Simeti, Mary Taylor. *Pomp and Sustenance.* New York: Alfred A. Knopf, 1989.

Sola, Pino. *Ricette e vini di Liguria.* Genoa: Sagep Editrice, 1993.

Willinger, Faith Heller. *Eating in Italy.* New York: William Morrow, 1998.

————. *Red, White & Greens.* New York: Harper Collins, 1996.

ACKNOWLEDGMENTS

Grazie to:

Evan Goldstein for his passion, wine knowledge, teaching skills, fine parenting, and loving support of his mother's work. ✻ At Chronicle Books, editor Bill LeBlond for his expertise, encouragement, and savoir faire; Sharon Silva for her usual amazingly thorough work; to Dinnick and Howells for their design; Vivien Sung for her art direction; Michele Fuller for enthusiastic support; and Amy Treadwell for patient editorial assistance. ✻ Kirsten Miller for her office expertise. ✻ Angela Wyant for her evocative photos of enoteca food; and Christine Masterson, who assisted her as food stylist. ✻ Carlo Petrini and the Slow Food organization for their passionate support of artisanal foods and dedication to regional culinary arts and traditions. ✻ Elizabeth Kane and Lavazza for sending me to Slow Food Salone del Gusto in 1998. ✻ Dun Gifford and Sara Baer Sinnott at Oldways for wonderful conferences in Italy where we ate and ate and ate and learned so much about food and culture. ✻ Fred Plotkin for taking me on that fabulous trip to Friuli. ✻ Dr. Ernesto Illy for his hospitality and friendship. ✻ Carol Field and Don Frediani for shared passion for all things Italian. ✻ For information and tastings, thanks to Susan Patton Fox at Ital-Foods; Paul Ferrari and Gianluca Guglielmi at A.G. Ferrari Foods; salami-maker Francois Vecchio; Peggy Smith and Sue Conley of Artisan Cheese; and Ari Weinzwig of Zingermans.

And to the sommeliers and enoteca proprietors who responded to my letter with recipes, menus, and information: Dario Laurenzi at Il Simposio at Enoteca Constantini in Rome ✻ Signora Cora at N'ombra de vin in Milano for sending suggested menus and wine pairings ✻ Renzo Franceschini at L'Enoteca Vino Vino in Terni and Oste della mal'ora in Orvieto ✻ Signora Luisa Lucia at Enoteca di Cormons ✻ Alessandra DeCandia at Enoteca DeCandia in Bari ✻ Raffaele Atzeni, Antica Enoteca Cagliaritana, Cagliari Sardinia ✻ Carlo Faccioli at Bottega del Vino Olinda Faccioli in Bologna ✻ Cristina Brunori at Enoteca Brunori in Jesi ✻ Giovanni Serrazanetti at Cantina Bentivoglio in Bologna ✻ Laura Marconcini at Lara Giulia Club in Sovigliana Vinci ✻ Alois Lageder at Vinoteque Lageder in Bolzano ✻ Mariarosaria Tagliaferri and Giovanni Sarais at Cantina Isola in Milano ✻ Simona and Roberto Gotti at Vineria Cozzi in Bergamo ✻ Pino Sola at Enoteca Sola in Genova ✻ Giovanni Rotti at Enoteca Giovanni in Montecatini Terme ✻ Salvatore Denaro at Il Bacco Felice in Foligno ✻ Marinella Migliori at Enoteca Migliori in Ascoli Piceno ✻ Franco and Simonetta del Gatto at Enoteca del Gatto in Anzio ✻ Guidi Luca at Osteria Vivaldi and chef Rudy Citon, Venice ✻ Sebastiano Mugnaini and Andrea Benetazzo at Enoteca al Volto in Venice ✻ Roberto Franceschini at Enoteca il Punto Divino in Viareggio ✻ Andrea Cecchini at Enoteca Regionale La Serenissima in Gradisca d'Isonzo ✻ Franco Larato at Enoteca Nonsolovino in Crema ✻ Emilio Baldi at Enoteca Vino Vino in Venezia ✻ Roberto Meneghetti at Osteria al Bacco in Venezia ✻ Le famiglie Saffiotti e Tamba at Cul de Sac, Roma ✻ Lino Stoppani at Peck Milano

INDEX

TABLE OF EQUIVALENTS

The exact equivalents in the following tables have been rounded for convenience.

LIQUID/DRY MEASURES

U.S.	METRIC
¼ teaspoon	1.25 milliliters
½ teaspoon	2.5 milliliters
1 teaspoon	5 milliliters
1 tablespoon (3 teaspoons)	15 milliliters
1 fluid ounce (2 tablespoons)	30 milliliters
¼ cup	60 milliliters
⅓ cup	80 milliliters
½ cup	120 milliliters
1 cup	240 milliliters
1 pint (2 cups)	480 milliliters
1 quart (4 cups, 32 ounces)	960 milliliters
1 gallon (4 quarts)	3.84 liters
1 ounce (by weight)	28 grams
1 pound	454 grams
2.2 pounds	1 kilogram

LENGTH

U.S.	METRIC
⅛ inch	3 millimeters
¼ inch	6 millimeters
½ inch	12 millimeters
1 inch	2.5 centimeters

OVEN TEMPERATURE

FAHRENHEIT	CELSIUS	GAS
250	120	½
275	140	1
300	150	2
325	160	3
350	180	4
375	190	5
400	200	6
425	220	7
450	230	8
475	240	9
500	260	10